PERMISSION TO BE
PERFECT

Books by Kyle Winkler

Shut Up, Devil
Permission to Be Imperfect

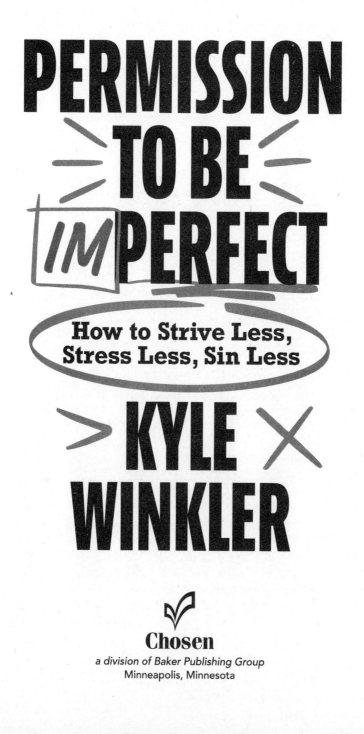

PERMISSION TO BE [IM]PERFECT

How to Strive Less, Stress Less, Sin Less

KYLE WINKLER

Chosen

a division of Baker Publishing Group
Minneapolis, Minnesota

Published by Chosen Books
Minneapolis, Minnesota
ChosenBooks.com

Chosen Books is a division of
Baker Publishing Group, Grand Rapids, Michigan

Printed in the United States of America

Library of Congress Cataloging-in-Publication Data
Names: Winkler, author.
Title: Permission to be imperfect : how to strive less, stress less, sin less / Kyle
    Winkler.
Description: Minneapolis, Minnesota : Chosen Books, a division of Baker Publishing
    Group, [2024] | Includes bibliographical references.
Identifiers: LCCN 2023036796 | ISBN 9780800763695 (paperback) | ISBN
    9780800762933 (casebound) | ISBN 9781493445059 (ebook)
Subjects: LCSH: Conduct of life. | Christian life.
Classification: LCC BJ1589 .W56 2024 | DDC 170/.44—dc23/eng/20230928
LC record available at https://lccn.loc.gov/2023036796

24   25   26   27   28   29   30   7   6   5   4   3   2   1

To those who try so hard
to be "normal" (whatever that is):

**HERE'S YOUR PERMISSION
TO BE YOU AND BE LOVED.**

Contents

Foreword

In an era when the rhythm of life is often measured by busyness, many of us lose sight of the serenity that comes with resting in God's embrace. Imagine enjoying divine relaxation, even amid the chaos. That's the invitation Kyle Winkler extends to each of us in his transformative book, *Permission to Be Imperfect*.

Are you one of the countless Christians darting about, ticking off spiritual checkboxes but feeling a void? That hollow sensation might just be the byproduct of a religion oversaturated with the "do more, be more" ethos. What if I told you this isn't about making heroic efforts to sustain a connection with God? Instead, it's about realizing the link has always been there, waiting for you to simply grasp it.

This book doesn't simply present theories or concepts; it unravels our very design, illuminating God's intentions for us. When we live in harmony with His design, the most profound discovery arises: an inspiring spiritual desire from within. Not the world's whims or fleeting passions, but a deep-seated yearning to live under the vast canopy of God's grace, liberated from the shackles of religious expectation.

In a world where the Bible belt often tightens its grip by pointing us to the Ten Commandments, Kyle bravely urges us to shift our gaze, to look solely to Jesus. The heart of this book isn't a set of rules. Instead, it's about letting God's grace rule. This timely message rings especially true in a generation witnessing droves walking away from the Church, where atheism is on the rise, and the image of God has been marred.

Kyle presents us with a refreshing elixir, offering an authentic portrayal of Christianity unclouded by misrepresentations. He's not simply adding to the conversation; he's rattling cages, challenging the status quo, and crying out for genuine change. Here, we aren't portrayed as sinners dangling precariously in the hands of an angry God, but rather as cherished saints cradled in the loving arms of our Heavenly Father.

In *Permission to Be Imperfect*, you'll rediscover God's unwavering love for you—a love that invites you to bask, to relish, and to find solace. With the Holy Spirit as our guide, Kyle nudges us toward the beautiful tenets of the new covenant of God's grace. He inspires us to embrace our true identity, to act unabashedly like children—children of God, reborn of the Spirit.

But how do you express Jesus without losing your essence? Kyle bridges this delicate balance, showcasing how our transformation isn't about adopting external rules, but stems from a profound DNA swap, which leads to a new heart, spirit, and an invigorating array of desires to now live from. Yes, we get to be ourselves and express Jesus at the exact same time.

As someone who has delved deep into the realms of God's grace in my own writings, I can't recommend Kyle's work enough. Because, dear reader, in this journey we call life, perfect performance isn't the goal—embracing God's perfect love is. So, dive in. The water's warm, and the grace is abundant.

Dr. Andrew Farley, bestselling author of *The Naked Gospel*, president at TheGraceMessage.org, and creator of BibleQuestions.com

1

The Divine Design

So God set another time for entering his rest, and that time is today. —Hebrews 4:7

"What more do I have to do?"

I begged, with a frantic frustration that sounded more like a desperate demand than an innocent inquiry, for God to give me an answer. I suppose it was desperate. After nearly a decade had passed since insecure, sixteen-year-old me dove headfirst into the faith, I felt more cheated than satisfied in my Christian life. With every passing day, the faith's promises of peace, joy, healing, deliverance, and victory seemed more like those of an as-seen-on-TV gadget. Those promises felt like the electric-shock, chiseled-ab-producing belt I once purchased from an after-midnight infomercial that sold me on an outcome it never delivered. Not even a bit.

When I say that I dove headfirst into the faith, I am not exaggerating. From early on, my understanding of the Gospel was that Jesus died to make me new, which included removing all the imperfections that had beset me since potty training. At least, if I maintained enough faith and applied the right principles to live like Jesus. So, armed with my Bible as an instruction manual, I set out to do my best.

The bustle of the first ten years of my faith makes recalling all the details a bit of a blur. The milestones are clear enough, though. I attended a Christian undergraduate school, gained employment in one of the fifteen largest churches in the country, climbed the ladder of leadership in another ministry, and then earned a master's degree in theology. In some seasons, I was inside of a church building every day. If I was not chasing conferences and revivals, I was learning or serving. Monday was spiritual growth seminar; Tuesday was advanced Bible study; Wednesday I was a youth leader; Thursday I cohosted a small group; Friday was prayer; Saturday and Sunday I attended services.

As I write, just beyond the brim of my laptop's screen is a bookshelf with at least a few shelves that harken me back to this era. With only a quick glance, I count several dozen Christian self-help books, some of which are volumes of prayer and deliverance strategies. Others are subtitled as ten-steps-to-this or twelve-steps-to-that. (I have moved at least twice since I have cracked open any of these books. Yet I continue to pack and unpack them, partly because my respect for books is such that I could never throw any away without feeling guilty. Maybe more than that, though, I suspect I have kept them unconsciously as a reminder of my journey.)

I do not mean to get lost down memory lane. Nor do I mean to belittle education, self-help books, or service. They all have their place. I am grateful for my education and the experiences that brought me here. My only purpose in recounting some of this is to demonstrate the extent of my effort in trying to get the faith to work. In those days, milestones, books, and roles served like dangling carrots toward that goal. My victory, healing, deliverance, or blessings were always just one "do this/apply this/achieve this" away.

That is until the day I crashed into the reality that I was ten years down the road and feeling far more exhausted than victorious. I had not changed into the extrovert that I hoped I would have. Remarks by friends and strangers still triggered reminders of childhood ridicule and rejection, plunging me into weeks of toxic thought and negative emotional patterns far more frequently than I care to admit. I had not defeated sin to the extent that I thought I should have, either. But now, added to the mix of my existing insecurities, failures, and flaws was a newfound fear of what it meant that I was not fixed enough.

Is there something wrong with me? I wondered nervously. *Is my faith real? Have I let God down?* Up until this point, "try harder" was the default answer to those questions.

Have you experienced the same? Can you, too, recount *everything* you have tried, yet concede to feeling more exhausted than energized? More depressed than joyful? More stressed than peaceful? More condemned than free? Do you grapple with the feeling that you somehow are not fulfilling your end of God's deal? Do you fear that He is gravely disappointed and holding back His promises—even His love— until you prove yourself worthy of them?

I know the feeling! I know the misery! As do many others. If you could spend a day with me to read the messages that fill my inboxes, you would see that the experience that I described is not yours or mine alone. Christians of every age write to me in fear of what it means that they still struggle with sin, symptoms, and shame despite their most valiant efforts to overcome. They beg to know the silver bullet that will end their battles. They clamor for more effective means to produce even a sliver of progress or persuade God to make good on a promise.

They wonder, "Could a different prayer strategy help? Is a longer, more rigid fast the answer? Should I be spending more time with God? Am I not mustering up enough faith?" If they have not already given up on the faith, many people live their faith based entirely on the question, "What more do I have to do?"

And therein lies the problem. It is not that God's promises are empty. The abundant, victorious Christian life is not like some mythical gold at the end of a rainbow that you can never reach. Nor is it only reachable by someone as pious as the pope. It is that most Christians live their lives all wrong, which is why they never experience what they expect. I know that is bold to say, but by the end of this book, you will understand why I can say it. For now, I will simply say that both religion and the world have mischaracterized God and grossly distorted what He wants from us. Because of these misrepresentations, most people launch into a well-meaning pursuit of pleasing God, doing things that only empower failure even more. Accordingly, we live life as if we are on a hamster wheel. That might be a good way to burn calories, but it is also a great way to burn out. And it is a horrible way to live.

God never intended for us to live under the constant pressure of trying to please Him, change ourselves, or produce

His promises. We are designed for something radically and refreshingly different. Something, dare I say, more effortless. There are several clues. The first comes from one of the most obvious places: how we are designed.

Clue #1: How We Are Designed

In the sixth grade, I joined my school's basketball team, albeit very reluctantly. It was my parents' idea, not mine. I suppose they thought I needed to do something other than lead Sonic the Hedgehog to safety on our Sega Genesis game console or dissect our Commodore 64 computer. Those were two of my go-to pastimes back then.

Team sports was not. At least not at school or in the presence of any kind of a crowd. At home, though, I could be decent. Well, that might be a stretch. Let's just say I could be okay. In our driveway, I could play a mad game of HORSE. (In case you are not familiar with this basketball game, it is played with two or more people, each who attempt to shoot a basketball from a place on the court that they hope the following person cannot match. Google it.) My signature shot in this game was from our front porch, behind two large evergreen bushes at least fifteen feet from the net. That shot often led me to victory.

But in the sixth grade, my ability at home could not translate to the fast-paced court surrounded by overly enthusiastic parents with signs and airhorns. In that situation, I could not even pass the ball correctly. Seriously. During my one and only game when the coach put me in, I only had to throw the ball from outside the court to a teammate inside. That should not have been a problem for someone who could make a swish from fifteen feet at home. Yet, with the feeling of all eyes on me, I passed the ball about five feet from my teammate . . . to no one! I choked. And I quit the team the next week.

My experience may be a bit exceptional, but choking under pressure is not. It is a well-documented phenomenon in the world of professional athletics. Speaking of basketball, studies reveal that professional players make free throws significantly more during training sessions than in games where the stakes are high. I doubt any have a problem passing the ball, but you get the point. It is the same for tennis players, golfers, and professionals of every sport. The more an athlete perceives that something is on the line, the higher the rate of failure.[1]

The reason is the same as to why brilliant students bomb a test, why interviewees go blank when asked a question they had memorized, why writers experience a mental block when up against a deadline, or why people struggle to recall the name of someone familiar when they need it most. Scientists observe that high-pressure moments, whether real or perceived, send the body into "danger mode" during which the brain produces a cocktail of stress-related hormones that impair memory and abilities. In this mode, the body attempts to shut down high-energy-consuming functions so that it can focus on survival. In other words, the higher the pressure, the more you are weakened physically.

Perhaps worse than the physical effect, though, is that pressure to perform also creates a toxic, emotional cycle of fear, shame, guilt, and self-doubt that makes it more likely that people will fail again and again.[2] This is the scientific evidence of the apostle Paul's spiritual observation that "law gives sin its power" (1 Corinthians 15:56). More on that in the next chapter.

My point is that people are not designed by God to live under high-stakes pressure. That is why the body interprets it as danger. Yet, this is precisely how most Christians live— not just in moments of necessity, but their entire lives. I did. Because of my distorted perception of both God and the Gospel, I believed I was saved by His grace but maintained by my performance. The stakes could not have been higher! Imperfect behavior meant that my salvation was at risk. Insufficient effort, discipline, or change meant that God was displeased. If God was displeased, then I feared He would not bless me, accept me, or love me. That meant I had to try harder.

Please hear this with the compassion that can come only from someone who has been there: if perfection or even near perfection is what you believe God desires from you, then you are living opposite of what God really desires. In this lifestyle, you will never realize the abundant, victorious life that God promises because you will buckle constantly under the pressure of trying to earn it or prove yourself worthy of it.

Sure, you may experience some success. And in those moments, you will think you are making progress . . . only to later pass the ball to thin air! The pursuit of perfection is unsustainable because it is impossible. You are not designed by God to live under the pressure of pleasing Him, changing yourself, or producing His promises. You are designed for something else. We just explored the first clue, which is in how we are designed. The second clue is even more telling: where we are designed to live.

Clue #2: Where We Are Designed to Live

Before ministry, I was a computer programmer. I learned to design web pages at age thirteen. In high school, I was employed professionally to code new projects. I attended college to study computers. Then, shortly after graduating, I made the dramatic switch to ministry. More than a decade of theology study and ministry did not kill my tech drive one bit, though. I still tune in faithfully for the new product announcements from my favorite companies. And though it is somewhat embarrassing to admit, I sometimes enjoy winding down in the evening to software tutorials on YouTube.

One thing that my technology passion seems to reveal is that I am wired naturally to relate to God as an intelligent designer, a programmer. This is why my teachings and books often include the occasional delve into science or biology. The last few pages are a case in point. The intentions of creators can be discerned by the design of their creations.

From the very genesis of my faith, I have considered the first couple of chapters of the Bible especially illuminating. The creation story that is found in these two chapters provides a snapshot of God's desire for His creation *without* the influence of sin. It reveals what I call "the divine design," which includes *where* God designed people to live, *how* He designed people to live, and the *benefits* of living according to His design.

The first insight that the Creation story offers toward this comes from the order in which God created. If you are familiar with the story, then you know that it describes the creation of everything in the heavens and the earth in six days. Each of these six days represents a milestone toward

His finished work in which a new category of things was brought to life. On day one, God created light, followed by the atmosphere on day two. God continued by creating land and plants on day three, then the sun, moon, and stars on day four. With the boundaries of the earth and sky established, God brought forth birds and sea creatures (day five), finishing with animals and humans on day six (see Genesis 1:1–27). After Creation was complete, the Bible records that God was pleased. Delighting in what He made, God declared it "very good" (Genesis 1:31) before resting on day seven (see Genesis 2:2).

What do the days of Creation have to do with God's design for how you and I live? Everything, really. You see, God's seventh day of rest was not like His other six days of Creation, which are each buttoned up with the statement "evening passed and morning came."

The seventh day is something special and eternal. It was the day that God blessed and declared holy. It was a day memorialized as *sabbath*, which I define as no labor, no striving, and no pressure.

The order of God's creation process is not coincidental; it is a clue that reveals His intentions for His people. Humankind was created *after* all the work was completed. Perhaps that is because God did not want any advice on how to do it! All joking aside, God formed humankind so that Sabbath was their first day. And not a "Sabbath day" that would set with the sun, but as the author of Hebrews revealed, a rest with no end (see Hebrews 4:1–11).

While the structure of Genesis 1 may be illuminating enough regarding God's divine design for humanity, Genesis 2 provides a close-up of the kind of life and relationship with Him that He envisioned for His people. This is made most evident in Genesis 2:8. "Then the LORD God planted a garden in Eden in the east, and there he placed the man he had made."

Humankind was made to live in Eden. So what? That is not news to most Christians. Yet Eden is the answer. Allow me to explain. When most people think of Eden, they think of a lush, tropical paradise at a constant 75 degrees with no humidity, no insects, and no mother-in-law. There is, however, more to Eden than what meets the eye. It is far more than merely the name of a perfect location. In the Hebrew language, Eden means "delight or enjoyment."[3] It is God's delight.

While I do believe that Eden was a real, physical place of bliss and enjoyment, it is also a place of enjoying God and being enjoyed by Him. Eden is symbolic of the position in which God created humankind to live. Simply put, in the beginning, God not only created people *out of* His delight, but He created people to live *in* His delight, where there is no pressure to perform or prove, no fear of disappointing or displeasing. Eden represents a place and position where God is simply pleased by our being, not our doing.

The Creation story continues to reveal what a pressure-free place based purely upon relationship with God produces. To help you better imagine it, I will repeat the verse we just explored, this time replacing "Eden" with "His delight."

Then the LORD God planted a garden in [His delight] in the east, and there he placed the man he had made. The LORD God made all sorts of trees grow up from the ground—trees that were beautiful and that produced delicious fruit.

Genesis 2:8–9

Do you see? Out of the ground of God's delight came beauty and delicious fruit. God's intention was that His people would not have to strive to make their environment beautiful, but beauty and the joy that comes from it would be a natural byproduct of the position in which He placed them. Beauty was a gift. So was provision. At a time when there was no need to eat the meat of animals, the first couple had all the nourishment they needed from fruit they did not labor to grow themselves. Though huge enough, beauty and fruit are not everything that came from God's delight. If you continue to read, you will see that the Bible also describes a river that flowed from Eden that kept both the Garden and the surrounding lands refreshed (see verse 10).

I know that I covered a lot of theology there, so please allow me to simplify what the Creation story reveals about God's design and intentions for His people. Adam and Eve were created after all the work was done. They did nothing to aid God in creating the universe. They were brought to life simply to enjoy God and be enjoyed by Him. Literally, their starting point was rest. And so was the basis of their existence and ongoing relationship with God. They did not have to work to produce beauty, blessings, or provision. They also did not have to convince God to produce them or prove to Him why they deserved them. Everything they needed grew effortlessly out of the ground of God's delight.

Please do not confuse laziness with God's intention for people. Shortly after Adam was created, the Bible clearly notes that God gave him a task. But again, replacing "Eden" with "God's delight" helps to clarify the extent of what God asked him to do. "The LORD God placed the man in the Garden of [God's Delight] to tend and watch over it" (Genesis

2:15). Yes, Adam was given something to do. But it was not to earn God's pleasure or to keep Him happy, but rather to cultivate delight, protect it, and keep it fresh.

By the end of this book, you will know what this means as it relates to your life today. The point for now is that the Creation story illustrates that humankind was not created to live *for* God's pleasure, but to live *in* and *from* God's pleasure. Hear that for yourself: you are not here to live *for* God's pleasure, but you are here to live *in* and *from* God's pleasure.

Break From the Pattern of the World

I know that some Christians vehemently oppose the idea that we are not created to live *for* God. I know this not only because I receive their messages, but because I was one of them for the first decade of my faith. I would have scoffed that this was some sort of "Christianity-lite" and gone on my way to pursue something deeper, something that required more sacrifice, more grit, more crucifixion. And I did, repeatedly. Until I tried everything with little to show for it, except exhaustion, fear, and shame. That is why I begged God to know, *What more do I have to do?*

That may be the most natural question to ask. After all, our culture is ruled by a system of perform-to-prove, do-to-get, achieve-to-succeed. From birth, our lives are lived as slaves to this pattern. It is no wonder, then, why anything less seems unnatural or even too good to be true. It is also no wonder why we mistake the character and expectations of God for the characteristics and expectations of the world, making Him out to be more like a taskmaster than the unconditionally loving Father that He is.

It is because of what this backward kind of lifestyle produces that the apostle Paul encouraged, "Do not conform to the pattern of this world" (Romans 12:2 NIV). Instead, friend, conform to the divine design. You are designed to live pressure free. You are designed to operate from a position of rest, not of earning. You are designed for Eden—the place where peace, joy, and all good things grow effortlessly. Doesn't that sound like a breath of fresh air compared to the way you have been living? Don't you at least *wish* it were true?

"Yes, but Eden is long gone!" you might be saying. "Adam and Eve were evicted from there. Their sin led to labor, striving, pressure, pain, and separation from God." That is true. After sin, the first couple had to leave the Garden. Yes, the physical location of Eden is long gone. It may be covered under hundreds of feet of mud because of Noah's flood. But what happened after that provides the next clue that Eden—the place and position of God's delight—is precisely where He prepared for us to return. Let's explore that next.

QUESTIONS FOR PERSONAL REFLECTION

1. What do you hope to get out of this book so that you are satisfied with it when you reach the end?
2. What do you believe is the goal of the Christian life? What have you been doing to pursue that goal? What so far are the physical, emotional, and spiritual results?

3. Consider your view of God's character. How has what you believe or have believed about Him influenced your life negatively?
4. How has the exploration of Eden changed your thoughts about God's expectations of you? What is it provoking you to reconsider about your lifestyle?
5. Does the idea that you are not created to live *for* God evoke feelings of hesitancy or hostility? Why or why not?

2

Why Diets Don't Work

Your strength comes from God's grace, not from rules . . . which don't help those who follow them. —Hebrews 13:9

The hours on my computer's clock seemed to pass like a snail through molasses. Each minute felt ten times longer than what it really was. At only eight in the morning, I knew it would be another long workday.

Time passed slowly because between every sentence of the article I was writing, my mind wandered to *what's for snack*, then *what's for lunch*, then *what's for snack*, then *what's for dinner*, then *what's for dessert*. For a few months, all I could think about was food. Not broccoli, kale, or cauliflower, either. Visions of Krispy Kreme donuts and Quarter Pounders danced through my head!

If you were to stalk my Facebook profile for photos of me back then, you would not find someone who looked overweight. I was more like something in the range of "skinny fat." This was back in the days before calorie counts were printed next to items on menus. So, honest to God, all throughout college I had no clue how many calories I consumed each time I made dinner out of a half dozen warm, original glazed donuts. If ignorance is bliss, then I was having a bliss-ard! At least until a few years out of college when I saw myself a bit pudgier in the cheeks than I preferred. Alas, it was time to take some action.

If you are old enough to remember the first decade of the twenty-first century, you might recall a plethora of fad diets that promised quick results. I suppose these quick-fix plans are not unique to the early 2000s, though. Humans have always wanted to shed weight fast. The only means to accomplish that is through some super-restrictive regimen. But this decade seemed especially characterized by these kinds of programs. In my young twenties, do you think I consulted a nutritional specialist? Not a chance. I single-handedly chose the diet that promised the most transformation in the shortest amount of time. Then off I went to do my best to stay away from all the good stuff it said not to eat. No more fried chicken. No more pizza. No more burgers. No more cheddar-garlic biscuits. No more glazed donuts!

To be fair to the program, the goal was not to restrict what you could eat for just a few months. It sought to instill a restrained lifestyle that would keep the weight off. The idea was that ninety days of food boundaries would teach the body to stop craving what is not good for it. That sounds reasonable, right? Most people think so. That is why the fad diet industry rakes in more than seventy billion dollars per year.[1]

These programs, of course, could not continue if they didn't produce results. And they do. There are people who lose weight quickly. I did. Though I did not have all that much to lose, I saw that just a few weeks of watching what I ate made a noticeable difference. The problem, though, is that the more I watched, the more I wanted to eat. The more I craved. Until I caved and had it. All of it. Admittedly, not long after the ninety days, I regained what I had worked so hard to lose.

Therein is the dirty little secret that the weight loss "machine" does not want people to know. And for years, perhaps the industry really did not know it themselves. I will give them the benefit of the doubt. But they certainly know it now. Studies uncovered that the more restrictive a diet is, the more it tends to backfire in the long term. The research finds consistently that around 95 percent of people who lose weight on restrictive diets regain it in one to five years. Sadly, most regain more than what was lost.[2]

The reason diets like this fail does not usually have much to do with a person's lack of willpower. They fail for one of two reasons that have to do with how humans are designed. The first reason relates to the "choking under pressure" principle that we explored in the last chapter. The pressure of constant restriction puts the body in danger mode, which triggers all kinds of mechanisms for survival that are counterproductive to goals, such as increasing hunger and storing fat.[3] The second reason has to do with how the brain is wired to attend to what is on the mind. Some call this the "power of suggestion." It is known scientifically as the "ironic process theory." Whatever the name, it is simply the age-old wisdom written in Scripture: your thoughts direct your actions (see Proverbs 4:23).

It was because of this principle that all the wrong foods were constantly on my mind during my diet. The program said to avoid carbs, so I thought of cheesy bread and sugar-coated bread. It said to stay far away from fried foods, so I battled wanting to cozy up to French fries, mozzarella sticks, and chicken nuggets. Chances are that you started to salivate upon reading the names of some of those snacks. Sorry! This is the power of suggestion at work, which has been a factor in our eating habits since the very beginning. It is what the enemy used on Adam and Eve to convince them to eat the fruit from the "tree of the knowledge of good and evil." He spoke frequently about its fruit, until they finally gave in and ate it (see Genesis 3:1–6). It all comes down to this: the more you try not to do something, the more likely it is that you will do it. That is at the core of how we are designed, which is why this affects far more than diets. In fact, anything based solely on "don'ts" is doomed for failure.

Don'ts Don't Work

Anyone who attended or had children in public (and some private) schools around the turn of the century likely remembers the D.A.R.E. program. Can you recall what the acronym stands for without going to Google? It was such a pervasive part of culture for a while that many people can easily remember it. Say it with me: Drug Abuse Resistance Education.

I was a participant in the D.A.R.E. curriculum during the seventh grade at my church school. I had no other choice, of course. Attendance was mandatory. For about four months, a group of police officers weekly visited my class, sometimes accompanied by the D.A.R.E. dog mascot himself. Or was it a lion? My memory fails me. Nonetheless, the program aimed to curb our interest in drugs and alcohol by the time we got to high school. This was a noble goal in my small, farming community. Besides running a pig's bladder down a cow pasture (aka playing football), drugs and alcohol were among the few other interesting options available to our high schoolers.

The officers did their best to scare us out of partaking anything not "kid tested, mother approved." We watched videos of real-life car accidents, reenactments, and plenty of photos of what we should not touch. I am sure you see where this is headed. The program failed miserably. Not just in my hometown, but across the nation.[4] The anti-drug emphasis did not make kids less likely to become addicts. Even worse, the consistent weight on just saying no tempted more kids to say yes.[5]

Because of its failure, D.A.R.E. was retooled into a positive-choice program with respectable results.[6] But why did nobody think to question its methods for so long? I suspect it is because we are used to controlling behavior through lists of don'ts. In my hometown and school this was the case. Even before I could read, ten of the most famous don'ts were instilled into me to memorize. Most know these as the Ten Commandments, which were chiseled by God's finger on stone tablets and given to Moses atop Mount Sinai (see Exodus 20:2–17).

The denomination in which I was raised stressed the Ten Commandments as the way to judge one's life and devotion. I thought of them as a gauge that indicated whether God is happy or mad at me at any given moment. Since we practiced regular confession of sin, knowing these commandments by heart also helped to know what to confess, especially as a kid. On more than one occasion, I nervously faced the priest with a blank stare. I knew I had committed at least one sin in the three months since my last confession. But for the life of me, as a third grader, I could not think of what it had been.

That is when the priest would ask me to recall the Ten Commandments. I began with the first: "You shall have no other gods before me." Being good on that, I continued to the second: "You shall make no idols." Since my Ninja Turtle action figures did not count, I saw no problem there. Commandment three usually got me, though: "You shall not take the name of the Lord your God in vain." I am sure I confessed that one with a half smirk, mostly because I was happy to find something to appease the priest so that I could get out of there!

To ensure we had the commandments down, our school frequently tested us on them. I suppose they feared that if we forgot them, it might send us into all-out rebellion, and we would end up sneaking in chocolate milk on a day other than Friday. (The administration believed that chocolate milk made kids hyper. So, it was a no-no, except on Fridays.)

Did the insistent emphasis on what not to do make my classmates and me perfect? Of course not. But did it make us behave better? For some of us, sure. But only at the expense of developing a pretty jacked-up perception of God, which arguably caused more harm than good later in life. That is a subject for the next chapter, though.

I am picking on the Ten Commandments because they are the most universal and revered set of don'ts to reference. It seems that nearly everyone raised in church, regardless of denomination, has some experience with them as I did. Even the unchurched have at least heard of them, if from nothing more than all the political fights to keep them displayed in government institutions.

What many do not know about the Ten Commandments, however, is that they are only the first 10 of a larger set of 613 laws given to Israel as a kind of code of ethics and conduct (collectively known as "the Law"). God had several good reasons to give these to His people, which we will explore momentarily.

But humans have a knack for making more out of something than is intended. People did this with the Law. Religious leaders believed that if laws were the way to godliness, then more laws must be the way to more godliness. Consequently, interpretations of interpretations of the original 613 dos and don'ts turned into thousands of human-made requirements that only bound the people with fear and condemnation. It was to these people, who were saddled with commandments on top of commandments, that Jesus gave His assurance, "Come to me, all of you who are weary and carry heavy burdens, and I will give you rest" (Matthew 11:28).

Through His life, death, and resurrection, Jesus came to fulfill the law of Moses because people could not live up to it themselves (see Matthew 5:17). He came to provide a means of permanent peace and godliness that no rule-following could ever produce. That is the Gospel message. Yet even some 2,000 years after Jesus accomplished this mission, I continue to see people baited into the Christian faith. They are given a promise of freedom, only to be handed a new set of don'ts that they are told are necessary to maintain their faith.

Sure, our contemporary requirements do not involve animal sacrifices as they did in the days before Jesus. Nor do they usually dictate that you cannot wear clothes made of both wool and linen. Thankfully, most people are not subjected to any of that. Still, many of us pick and choose some of the less radical rules by which we judge ourselves and others.

For many years, I did. As a newly born-again Christian, tattoos were unquestionably off-limits. So was merely being in the presence of alcohol. But I also judged my godliness by the amount I committed to otherwise healthy spiritual practices, such as Bible reading, prayer, fasting, and church attendance. Like the religious leaders in Jesus' day, I erred on the side that more is better and makes God happier. Better safe than sorry, I believed. Except that belief caused me to live sorry, never feeling safe, which only made me worse, never better.

I am sure you can recount some of your own items from a "what-it-takes-to-be-a-real-Christian" list. Some people are judged according to the way they pray. Some are judged according to the Bible version they use. Others are convinced that Christianity requires unwavering devotion to certain political ideologies. Perhaps you were made to believe that a "real Christian" does not send their child to a public school. One lady shared with me that her church dictated that women may only wear pink or white fingernail polish. I imagine that she struggled with an intense temptation to wear blue!

As I said last chapter, our culture programs us with rules from the moment we leave the womb. But some folks subconsciously grow to like them, too. Rules and boundaries provide a kind of safety because they take the guesswork out of how to live and how to please God. But as we observe in societies and governments, safety always comes at the expense of freedom and abundant life.

Sure, as with diets and anti-drug programs, strict adherence to restrictions provides results and offers a sense of comfort in the short term. Satisfying rules can make you feel really successful for a while. Until you inevitably miss the mark, and then you feel really lousy. The guilt of failure compounded with the pressure to perform makes the one who lives by the letter of the law more susceptible to failure, not less. That is precisely why the apostle Paul warned that "those who depend on the law to make them right with God are under his curse" (Galatians 3:10).

Why Did God Lay Down the Law?

For those who measure their status with God according to how well they follow rules, failure always leads to shame. This started with the first couple. After they succumbed to the enemy's temptation, Adam and Eve hid from God in fear of how He might respond. God never asked for this response. Nor did He ever provide a reason for them to react accordingly. I suspect the enemy had something to do with this. As he still does today.

While the first couple hid in the bushes, God searched for them. Hide-and-seek with God is futile, of course. He knew their whereabouts all along. But His search demonstrates His heart to pursue even the most broken. Though the first couple was responsible for no small failure (only the corruption of God's entire creation!), God did not send them away with a list of what not to do or touch. After making them aware of the realities of life in a fallen environment, God covered their shame and tasked angels to guard the tree of life so that they could not eat from it again and thereby regain eternal life (see Genesis 3:22). This was not punishment; this was mercy. God protected them from the misery of living forever in a fallen condition.

As the Bible teaches, the inevitability of failure gets passed down from generation to generation. Nobody can escape it. Excuse the pun, but when it came to Adam and Eve's children, the apple did not fall far from the tree. In a moment of envy, their son Cain killed his younger brother, Abel. Amazingly, though, God demonstrated mercy yet again. He sent Cain away with supernatural protection from those who might want to avenge for Abel's death (see Genesis 4:15).

How God desires to relate to humanity is revealed clearly in the first few chapters of Genesis. Not through rules and punishment, but with love, mercy, and grace. So, what happened? Why did God eventually throw the book at His people with such burdensome commandments? Did He have a change of heart? Far from it. There are several reasons, which lead back to what He always intended for us.

First, in the days of Cain and Abel, people did whatever seemed right in their own eyes because they did not yet have a standard of right and wrong. People compared themselves to each other and figured if so-and-so got away with murder, so should I. Since humans had little clue as to what was best for them, God made it clear. He laid down the law, so to speak, spelling out sin in no uncertain terms (see Romans 5:13, 20; Galatians 3:19).

As we are learning in our contemporary culture, subjective truth plunges a society into chaos. It does not take all that long for a society like this to destroy itself. After only 1,600 years since Adam and Eve's first sin, unrestrained wickedness not only pervaded the culture, but evil consumed the thoughts of people (see Genesis 6:5). God sought to cleanse the world of this depravity and begin again with a handful of better-behaved people.

That is the story of Noah's flood. Yet, given enough time, even good people make bad choices. Not long after Noah, the sin cycle with its natural consequences once again ran amok. Accordingly, God set His Commandments in stone as a kind of guardian (see Galatians 3:23–25). The rules helped to restrain sin and preserve God's people until Jesus arrived to deal with sin once and for all.

Ultimately, God established the Law to show people that they cannot save themselves through their own actions (see Romans 5:19–20; Hebrews 10:1–4). Because of the weakness of the flesh, God knew that the more people are told what not to do, the more they will do it. He also knew that pressure to perform only leads to failure. This is what the apostle Paul meant when he explained that "the law gives sin its power" (1 Corinthians 15:56). "Thou shall nots" were never meant to produce anything good. Not righteousness. Not peace. Not even good behavior. They were always meant to both expose human imperfection and to produce more and more failure until people realized that they could not please God on their own.

Not everyone got it back then. Nor does everyone get it today. Yet nothing is better than rules to get people to arrive at this realization. It brought me to it. I suspect you are reading this book because you have realized this, too. Living up to rules should lead to exhaustion and frustration because that is God's design. All so that you will surrender the pursuit of perfection to find lifelong rest in Jesus who restores you to Eden, which is the center of God's delight.

The Way That Works

Please do not confuse everything I said so far as justification to throw caution to the wind. It is not. Undoubtedly, God set boundaries and outlined the way He intends for things to be and work most effectively regarding all kinds of situations in life. Certainly, treating people respectfully, being honest, and eating healthy foods prevent many headaches (and body aches). It is wise to avoid some things. I do not advocate for spiritual anarchy or an anything-goes lifestyle. That is a sure way to bondage, not victory.

Still, the way to victory is also not as it is often prescribed to many Christians today. You will not grow and thrive in an environment where meticulous adherence to rules is the means to prove or achieve anything. A life focused on rule following is what the apostle Paul called "the old way," which for all the reasons we explored, "brings condemnation" (2 Corinthians 3:9). God's people lived bound to dos and don'ts for about 1,500 years, and nobody achieved perfection through them. Nor was anybody saved by following them even as best as they could. This kind of rule following served only to bring about what Paul revealed is "the new way, which makes us right with God!"

What is this new way? It is a way in which "grace rules instead" (Romans 5:21). It is a way pioneered by Jesus in which imperfections, flaws, and failures do not count you out of God's affection, His promises, or His family. The new way is a life lived by the Gospel truth that you have permission to be a work-in-progress, which is permission to be imperfect. That kind of freedom fosters a pressure-free environment that produces far more victory than being obsessively careful of what not to do (see Hebrews 13:9).

Here again, we should not be surprised to see that this spiritual principle of permission is reflected in our natural world. Going back to weight loss, while yes, consuming fewer calories is important, studies continue to show that a permission-based approach is far more effective than one of restrictions. I am not a dietitian, nor am I prescribing any weight loss plan, but years of research bears that plans that teach a healthy mindset of pleasurable eating, which includes the foods you love, are what work in the long term.[7] The point is, success happens when the pressure to be perfect is removed.

Speaking of following a "way," my first snow skiing lesson provided practical wisdom that would have saved me much grief had I understood it spiritually back then. It came on a cold January night in 2001. My new church youth group bussed a couple dozen of us teens to St. Louis, Missouri, for an overnight ski trip. In case you are wondering, St. Louis is not known for skiing. We would not be whizzing whimsically through acres of powdery snow. This place offered about a half-dozen slopes that split off from the top of a single hill covered in man-made stuff that was more like sleet.

From the lodge at the bottom, I stared up at that hill in awe. I stood there frozen for a minute (literally!), mesmerized by the skiers weaving in and out of pine trees and massive metal poles as they zoomed down the hill. "Maybe one day," I remarked to a friend. I expected to stay on the bunny slope all night where I began my first lesson.

It was less than an hour before I got the hang of keeping my balance on the skis and made it across that bunny slope without a tumble. With more than six hours left in the evening, the instructor sensed some of us would get bored there. He offered some advice to those brave enough to try the hill. I listened intently.

"As you ski down the hill, don't look at the trees or the poles," he warned. "Focus on the open path in front of you." One of the extroverts in our group begged to know why. "You will hit what you focus on," is all he had to say for us to get it. Less than an hour later, I heeded his advice and made it down that hill safely dozens of times.

Since that lesson at sixteen years old, I have discovered that this instruction is not only wisdom for skiers, but for anyone who needs to make quick maneuvers. In learning to fly or to drive or to play video games, it is taught: "Look where you want to go, not at what you want to avoid."[8] The same ought to be taught as Christianity 101. Rather than living while concentrating on what not to do, focus on the way of grace that is before you. That way is lined with unconditional love. That is the path of lasting victory. The first step on that path is to see God as He really is. Let's look at that next.

QUESTIONS FOR PERSONAL REFLECTION

1. Have you ever tried a self-improvement program based on restrictions? What did it feel like throughout? What were the long-term results?

2. Is your Christian life more focused on what not to do than it is on grace and freedom? What influenced that focus?

3. According to what laws or spiritual practices have you judged yourself or others? What made these important to you?

4. Considering that God established the Law to reveal the need for a Savior, what effects might this have on how you relate to yourself and others?

5. In what areas of your life do you long to experience victory? In these areas, what might a grace-based approach look like?

3

Get a New God

God is love, and all who live in love live in God,
and God lives in them. —1 John 4:16

"I have discovered God's name! His *real* name!" I beamed to
my fellow thirteen-year-old neighbor while rinsing my hands
under our kitchen faucet.

"Oh yeah?" she quipped, turning to face me with a smirk of
unbelief. But I was serious. I believed that I had uncovered a
secret about God that was hidden in plain sight in Scripture
but somehow had been missed by almost everyone else.

After a few second pause to dry my hands and build tension for this epic unveil, I looked up and answered, "Hallowed." That was not what she expected. In fact, she did not
even know what it meant. But she took the same religion
classes I did, so I knew she would understand as soon as I
quoted the first line in the Lord's Prayer.

"You know," I urged, "Jesus prayed, 'Our Father in heaven,
hallowed be your name'" (Matthew 6:9 ESV).

I promise that I did not just string you along to the punch line of a dad joke. (Though I do have plenty of those!) I really believed this, at least for a few days. When I was in the seventh grade, my parents finally relented to my insistence that we subscribe to the internet. For an introvert like me, this was a dream! In the days of dial-up connections, I tied up our phone line for hours every night exploring this new world. Sometimes it led me to all kinds of fake news, well before that term became overused. This "discovery" was one of them.

I believed a lot of wrong things about God back then, some of which continued for years later. His name was the least problematic of them. Far worse was my belief (or my ignorance) about His character and how He related with people. Yes, some of my misconceptions came because of articles or videos I had seen on the internet. There was one website that offered booklets of cartoons that each told a story intended to draw people to the faith. Though I am not sure that *draw* is the right word—*scare* is more like it. The cartoons always drew God as a stern old man with a long, white beard. I swear that in some of them He held a gold trident with lightning bolts that shot out from its three prongs. I could be imagining that. But it fits with the bumper sticker they offered, which warned, "Jesus is coming back, and boy is He mad!"

I wince rereading that last line. Back then, though, I never thought anything of this angry-God portrayal. It affirmed what I already believed about Him, which was passed down to me by religion teachers, portrayed to me through the stoic statues that lined the walls of my childhood church, and promoted to me as the reason for natural disasters. They called them acts of God. I heard some indignant television preachers assert that these acts of God were God's wrath against certain people groups.

Like I said, confusing God's name was the least of my problems. What was devastating as I matured is that I saw God as a schizophrenic taskmaster who kept meticulous notes on everyone's behavior. Accordingly, I believed that He loved me if I obeyed the rules and did my part in all the spiritual disciplines. But He had a short fuse that could ignite quickly if I did not prove that I was improving myself. I sometimes feared that He hated me because of my imperfections.

I was not alone in my fear that was rooted in misconceptions of God's character. It grieves me to say this but still today, I find that most people see God the way I once did, for similar reasons as I once did. Sadly, what the apostle Paul observed in the early days of the Church is just as true now. The enemy has blinded the minds of people so that they are unable to see the true character of God, and therefore, never receive His Good News (see 2 Corinthians 4:4). Both outside and inside of the Church.

Giving Up God

Since the time I was deceived about God's name, more than 25 years ago, the internet articles have not gotten any better. Age-old misconceptions continue to malign His character with devastating effects on people and culture. A headline on a political shock jock's website caught my attention recently. It blared, "I Propose We Give Up God."[1]

Bold, I thought to myself. *I wonder what this is about.* Just two sentences in, I knew. It was yet another commentary on how awful God is to cause such suffering in the world. One of the words the author used to describe Him was *hateful*.

As the book of Ecclesiastes reminds us, "There is nothing new under the sun" (Ecclesiastes 1:9 ESV). People have blamed God for every sorrow under the sun for millennia. Even the people God brought miraculously into the Promised Land did. In more than one instance, this led King David to remark, "Only fools say in their hearts, 'There is no God'" (Psalm 14:1; 53:1). Many take this as a knock at atheism. But there was no unbelief in David's day. His comments refer to a people who lost faith in God's goodness because they mistook their trials as a sign of God's abandonment.

While atheism was not a thing back then, it is now. Not surprisingly, confusion about God's character tops the list of reasons why people choose atheism. In his book *The God Delusion*, renowned atheist Richard Dawkins scoffed, "The God of the Old Testament is arguably the most unpleasant character in all of fiction."[2] Through his books and interviews, Dawkins's derogatory comments about God embolden many who once hid their unbelief. My social media feeds are vandalized occasionally by his followers, who all seem to think that they are the first to refer to God as Dawkins does, "the flying spaghetti monster."[3]

Publicly, atheists like to cite science as the reason that they reject God. But when you get an unbeliever one-on-one, his or her reasons are often based on what the unbeliever sees in the Old Testament, which he or she then assumes is the cause of suffering today. Many Christians do not do much to help. Some only continue to perpetuate and reinforce a monstrous view of God.

46

I once lived in a town where a group of legalists took to street corners each Sunday to wave signs at passersby that expressed how God hates this or that kind of person. I know that even these sign-wavers are loved by God, but I confess that words worse than "fools" came to my mind as I passed.

Legalistic demonstrations of God, often spread by people who claim to love Him, not only contributed to the rise of secularism, but also to a recent movement known as deconstructionism. If you have not yet heard of this, think of deconstruction as it is most basically defined. It is the breakdown of a system. In the case of faith, deconstruction is about analyzing and unraveling long-held beliefs, doctrines, and ideologies. Our internet age is ripe for this kind of movement, whereby polarizing thoughts are argued one on top of the other in a social media feed.

To be sure, deconstruction is not always bad. One might say that this book is a kind of deconstruction. If your faith and perspective of God is built on misconceptions, it is good to tear down those toxic beliefs—as long as you rebuild your faith with truth. The problem is that many end up deconstructing their way out of belief entirely and giving up on God. This is tragic. I know that many horrors have been (and still are) committed in God's name. It is no secret that some Christians weaponize Him and His Word to shame people who desperately need His Good News. The gravity of that makes me tremble as I write. The answer, however, is not to give up God. It is to get a new God.

Since your nose is in this book, I assume that you do not identify as someone "unchurched" or "dechurched." The thought of giving up God probably never crossed your mind. But do you wrestle with giving up on yourself? On your dreams? On your worth? Do you battle insecurity, shame, stress, anxiousness, fear, or discouragement? These symptoms may be telltale signs of unbelief in the true character of God, even if it is only partial unbelief or unbelief out of ignorance. Twentieth-century theologian A. W. Tozer acknowledged this when he said, "What comes into our minds when we think about God is the most important thing about us."[4] In other words, what you believe about God affects everything in your life, from how you act to how you see yourself. That is why the enemy is committed to keeping people blinded to God's true character.

As I explored in my book *Shut Up, Devil*, the name *devil* in Greek means "slanderer."[5] To slander means to lie for the purpose of destroying someone's character. This is what the devil does in our minds. He first attempts to destroy God's character, then he attempts to destroy your character. The worry that God is withholding leads to distrust. The belief that God afflicts fans the flames of fear. The suspicion that God does not care develops depression. I could go on. So many of our most toxic emotional, psychological, and spiritual symptoms are the byproducts of an incorrect or incomplete answer to the question, "Who is God?" It is for this reason that, even for committed Christians, the answer to many of life's issues is to get a new God—which is to say, get a new perspective of Him.

The Making of a Mean God

Have you ever tackled a year-long read through the Bible? Though there is nothing spiritual about my timing or structure, when I commit to a plan like this, I like to begin on

January 1 and work my way from front to back. No jumping around for me. My linear way of thinking would not allow that.

A Bible-reading plan like mine will get you to the New Testament sometime in October. If you make it until then. The Old Testament gets grueling and depressing if you do not know how to see it properly. For years, I did not. I have found that most atheists, skeptics, legalists, and well-meaning Christians do not, either. Since the Old Testament makes up nearly 75 percent of the Bible, its depiction of God often makes up the majority of how people see Him. And in it, let's be honest, God does not look all that great. He seems mostly mean, vindictive, and jealous. Richard Dawkins would add a "malevolent bully."[6] Fair enough, Dick. There is no escaping how God comes across in the Old Testament. But we should not build our conclusions about God's character based upon it, either. That is because the Old Testament describes God incompletely.

Did that just cause you to pause? To be clear, I do not mean that the Old Testament is not accurate. This is not an attack on its validity or inspiration. God's character in the Old Testament is incomplete because it is clouded by the effects of sin and described by people who did not have the full picture of things. As a result, the Old Testament characterizes God as largely wrathful and angry, responsible for both the good and the bad, and impossible to please. Some of this description is true, some of it is not. Now, please give me a chance to escape the corner I just backed myself into.

As we explored in the last chapter, sin grew to levels that not only threatened the physical health of people but also the health of the world. The greater danger, however, was that sin threatened to destroy the people from whom ultimate redemption would come, which risked eternal separation from God for all of humanity. Sin had to be restrained in radical ways until the time was right for its power to be taken away forever. A set of rules that was impossible to keep was one of God's methods of restraining sin. But what was not controlled with rules had to be consumed (sometimes in grand displays) by wrath. That was never a pleasant sight; but, to protect what was to come, it was necessary.

True as God's anger burned toward sin at times, in the Old Testament, not every comment about God or interpretation of events is true. That is because, until almost six hundred years before Jesus, scholars say that God's people did not know about Satan as an evil enemy who was independent of God.[7] Back then, he was believed to be one of God's angels, sent to serve His purposes. This is evident from the beginning. Consider that Adam and Eve did not see the devil in the serpent. They simply believed that the serpent was a creature made by God to test their faithfulness (see Genesis 3:1). It was not identified as the devil until the New Testament era (see 2 Corinthians 11:3; Revelation 12:9). Consequently, much of the Old Testament is written from the perspective that every trial and tragedy is sanctioned and sent by God.

Is it true that the events described in the Old Testament happened? Absolutely. Did everyone in those days interpret them all correctly as coming from God's hand? Absolutely not. The story of Job may be the best example of what incomplete information leads people to conclude about God. Do you know the story?

In a series of tragedies, Job lost almost everything except his nagging wife. Yes, with the benefit of hindsight and divine inspiration, the author of the book of Job saw the devil in the details. But all along, Job believed it was God who was doing the taking. "The LORD gave, and the LORD has taken away" (Job 1:21 ESV). Later, Job's friends mistook his tragedies for God's punishment. In the end, they were corrected by God for defaming His character (see Job 42:7).

Is it true that Job suffered great losses? Of course. Is Job's assertion that God gives and takes away true? Not entirely. Yes, God gives. He is always the giver of anything that is good. Thankfully, God's people knew that then and we still know that today (see Psalm 85:12; James 1:17). But Job misunderstood who caused his suffering. He assumed it was God; we know it was the devil.

I know that everything I just said is a big idea. I encourage you to study it on your own. But at least consider it as you read the Old Testament. There is no doubt that many things you see in it are God's swift responses to sin. But some of what you read is an incomplete description of God by people who did not have all the information.

The Greatest Discovery

When you read the Old Testament, keep in mind that you are not reading merely a history book of facts. Yes, it is factual. But it is richer than that. The Old Testament is the inspired story of God's relationship with people. When you read it, you are peering into the moments of people on a journey of discovery. Had God wanted us to know everything about Him or His creation, He would have programmed us with all wisdom from the beginning. Instead, He seems to delight in leading us to truths at the right time. Even though it means that He often gets blamed for things He should not.

The root of evil is one of the fundamental truths that humans received along our journey. We were later led to truths about the natural causes of things like gravity, viruses, and thunderstorms. Even in those things, of course, we do not know everything. Still, each time we come to some new revelation, I like to think that God celebrates our progress. I imagine Him huddled with His angels, giddy about what we found and where we are going. Whatever the case, far more than uncovering how creation works, the greatest truth He unveiled—the discovery that He delights in the most—is His true character. "God is love" (1 John 4:8).

Certainly, God's people always knew that love is an attribute of God. But it took some 4,000 years to know that love is His very essence. The New Testament revealed this to us, adding that God at Creation was Jesus, who is described as "full of unfailing love and faithfulness" (John 1:14). This is another way of saying that God is full of grace. He always has been. In hindsight, we can see all the clues that lead up to His great reveal. It only makes sense that God would create us to respond best to His true character.

As we already explored, our bodies are designed for Eden, which is a place of pure grace. God related to people with grace before sin. And He continued to relate to people with grace well after the first sin. Grace covered Adam and Eve's nakedness. Grace protected Cain after he killed his brother. Grace blessed Abraham and Sarah with a child despite their lack of faith. Grace kept God present with Moses through his insistent doubts.

Until the Law was given through Moses, the Bible contains more examples of grace than I have the space to tell. One more reality to consider is the fact that, in those days, sin did not repel God's presence as if it were more powerful. I know that this is contrary to many of today's teachings. Surely you have heard that God cannot be in the presence of sin. Yet, for many years, He was. Until He gave the Law through Moses, God continued to be present among very imperfect people. That is because He chose to relate with them according to grace.

With the institution of the Law, things changed. God began to hold people accountable for their sins (see Romans 5:13). We have already explored the good reasons why. This did not change His nature; it just changed how people saw and related to Him. During this time, God chose to relate through His attribute of justice with occasional glimpses of grace. He continued to rescue Israel after their blatant acts of rebellion. Though they were sometimes punished for those acts. It was never God's intention to relate to humanity with a split personality like this, though. That is why God provided them with clues to a future of pure grace and a return to His delight. One of the most obvious came through the prophet Isaiah. "For I will not fight against you forever; I will not always be angry" (Isaiah 57:16).

God Fully Revealed

Throughout the Bible, it seems that one of God's favorite miracles is to open the wombs of women who are unable to conceive. He loves to bring life out of situations that appear hopeless. He also seems to enjoy surprising people who draw

53

the wrong conclusions based solely on human knowledge. After thousands of years of law, He revealed one of the most undeniable clues about His true character to the world in this way.

As the story goes, a woman named Elizabeth could not become pregnant with her husband, Zechariah (see Luke 1:5–7). The best minds of their time wrote it off as impossible. I know friends and family members who were given similar news. Several have shared how difficult it is to hear pregnancy announcements from those who get pregnant with far less effort. I cannot imagine how unfair it must feel. It must have seemed especially unfair for Elizabeth and Zechariah. The Bible is sure to note that they both came from a line of priests and lived "careful to obey all the Lord's commandments and regulations" (Luke 1:6). If anyone had deserved the blessing of a child, it was them.

Then, one day, Zechariah received news that their devotion had paid off! While performing his priestly duties in the temple, the angel Gabriel appeared to him with this life-changing announcement: "Your wife, Elizabeth, will give you a son, and you are to name him John" (verse 13). Zechariah must have been elated. Their prayers would be answered! Yet he was also flummoxed. Everyone said it was impossible. He wondered aloud, "How can I be sure this will happen?" (verse 18). That question rendered him speechless. Literally. Hearing Zechariah's unbelief, Gabriel reprimanded him. "Since you didn't believe what I said, you will be silent and unable to speak until the child is born" (verse 20).

At first glance, it appears that Gabriel punished Zechariah. But the benefit of hindsight reveals something fascinating. You see, a first-born child was traditionally named after his father. That is why, shortly after Elizabeth gave birth, family and friends were bewildered as to why they did not name the baby Zechariah. Though it was none of their business, like typical family members, they argued as though it was. When Elizabeth refused to budge on her decision to name the baby John, they turned to Zechariah for help. "What say you, oh man of the house?" Perhaps Zechariah's speechless condition had scared him into obedience. But he was obedient, nonetheless. The crowd was stunned when he wrote on a tablet, "His name is John." They were stunned again when Zechariah's mouth reopened instantly to praise God (see verses 61–64).

To appreciate the drama that surrounded John's name, you must understand what was in a name back then. A name was not merely a label to call someone—it held spiritual significance. It was a job description that often was prophetic of one's destiny. This is especially true of John, which means "God is gracious."[8] Considering that John was the cousin and forerunner of Jesus, his name was soberly chosen by God. That is probably why He went to such lengths to ensure it happened.

At the time of John's birth, people attempted to understand the meaning behind the supernatural events that unfolded. Yet until Luke told the story in his gospel, I do not think they arrived at perhaps the most significant conclusion. Both Elizabeth and Zechariah were pictures of the Law. Though they had done everything right, they were unable to produce life on their own. Yet God filled their barren and hopeless womb with life. And that life was the announcement that God is gracious. In the same way that the Law had always pointed to Jesus, it did in this circumstance, too.

If this were the only announcement of its kind, you may be tempted to brush it aside as happenstance. But the clues kept coming, faster and more revealing. Nearly every feature of the Christmas story—from Bethlehem to the manger to the shepherds—is prophetic of what was to come. Perhaps the clearest one, however, is the angelic announcement given to those shepherds upon His birth. Heaven was waiting anxiously for this, it seems.

With prophecies fulfilled and humankind ready, the time had come for God to end the clues and reveal who He really is in a way that could not be missed. Born in a manger, Unfailing Love took on flesh. The angels broadcast what that meant with a radiance that eclipsed the night sky. "Glory to God in the highest, and on earth peace, good will toward men" (Luke 2:14 KJV).

Do not mistake the peace that the angels harkened as peace in a worldly sense, void of trials and tragedies. (Although, it was a burgeoning realization that God was not responsible for them in the future.) Ultimately, the angels proclaimed that God had come to earth in the flesh to make a way for permanent peace between God and people.

If that is not awe inspiring enough, just as God used John's name to announce the return of grace, He used him again thirty years later to elaborate on how it would happen. When it came time to begin His public ministry, Jesus came to the Jordan River to be baptized by His cousin John. As their eyes met, John's spirit leapt inside of him, accompanied with a pent-up bellow: "Behold, the Lamb of God, who takes away the sin of the world!" (John 1:29 ESV). Like peeling an onion, God led people on a journey through the ages to discover who He really is, layer by layer. In many ways, it was a journey back to Eden.

Some of us are still on this journey, though that can end now. What God wants people to know is that He is not the mean, vindictive, jealous, malevolent bully characterized by those who did not or do not know the whole story. But God is gracious, comprised of unfailing love. It is, of course, one thing to hear God described in this way by announcements and prophecies. It is another to encounter His true character as it was demonstrated perfectly in the flesh as Jesus. The discovery continues. You'll see it in the next chapter.

QUESTIONS FOR PERSONAL REFLECTION

1. Before reading this chapter, how did you see God? What attributes about Him are dominant in that view?

2. What events, situations, teachings, or people in your life influenced any negative perspectives that you might have about God?

3. Consider that sin is not more powerful than God's presence. Does this differ from what you have heard? How might this truth affect your relationship with God positively?

4. God always works in us to reveal more about Himself. Identify some moments in your life when God's character became clearer to you.

5. From what you have discovered in this chapter, has your view of God changed? If so, describe it in your own words.

4

What Did Jesus Do?

So the Word became human and made his home among us. He was full of unfailing love and faithfulness. —John 1:14

The possibilities for ministry these days are as exciting as they are endless. In our digital age, we can speak to countless people on the other side of a screen, many of whom would never step foot in a church. Like any convenience, the "other side of a screen" has downsides, too, which are not always fun or fruitful. Screens give people a sense of courage to say what they never would in person. With comment boxes below everything on social media, it is too easy for people to speak their mind with no inhibitions.

Like I said in the last chapter, my content occasionally attracts the scoffs of militant unbelievers. I do not know why they waste the only existence they believe that they have on arguing faith. But I kind of expect antagonizing comments from them. Far more frustrating to me are the armchair theologians who pick apart a 280-character tweet for not mentioning every possible caveat. I especially attract vitriol from these people anytime I mention God's goodness and love. "But, but, but," they gush like a goat, followed by their reasons for why my words cannot be true.

One lady was irate over a video I shared about how radically God loves. "Stop commonizing God! He is holy!" she screamed in all caps. (It is human to want to defend yourself. And sometimes I prove myself especially human in that regard. Though, these days, I am better at resisting the immediate impulse to prove them wrong. Instead of responding online, I write books. That is far more satisfying to me.)

Essentially, the lady was angry because I said that God is not angry. I never said that God is not holy. Nor would I ever even hint at that. Undoubtedly, God is holy. But in her mind (and in other minds like hers), His holiness is equated with how strictly He enforces the rules and how enraged He gets when people break them. I get it. I used to believe that way, too. It might be from my upbringing, but the word *holy* just sounds somber and gloomy to me. There are still times when hearing it triggers a sense of guilt, which I push aside because I know better. The word *holy* simply means "uncommon."[1]

Have you discovered yet that being angry is not all that uncommon? I rediscover this almost every day as I brave Interstate 4 in Central Florida, where I live. People are not so kind in the rat race to the house of mouse (aka Walt Disney World). I am sure drivers are not that different where you live. Wrath and rage are common. What would be uncommon is to love that maniac who cut you off.

Jesus said the same. At the beginning of His ministry, He shocked a Jewish crowd when He equated God's perfection with unconditional love for everyone. And I do mean shocked. Imagine being one of them. As a Jew, your life re-volved around following the Law and all the interpretations of it. You were taught that God demands separation from certain people, such as Samaritans, tax collectors, and lepers. Then one day, in a single talk, this otherworldly, miracle-working rabbi challenges almost everything you know about God. I am describing to you Jesus' renowned Sermon on the Mount (see Matthew 5).

In the middle of His sermon, Jesus remarked, "You have heard the law that says, 'Love your neighbor' and hate your enemy" (verse 43). He was good at baiting their attention like this. In a short time, His disciples learned that His instigating remarks were often followed with a wrecking ball to their worldview. This time was no different. Jesus continued, "But I say, love your enemies! Pray for those who persecute you!" (verse 44). This was radical. Loving people on the far end of the spectrum meant loving everyone, period. He continued to reveal that this is precisely what God does, and it is what makes Him good and perfect. Jesus urged the audience to have the same heart. "Be perfect, even as your Father in heaven is perfect" (verse 48).

To be sure, Jesus did not say all of this to raise the bar with another impossible law to follow. A call to flawless-ness was not His point. Like most of His Sermon on the Mount, His words served to confront both their sense of self-righteousness and their idea of who God is. His point was to challenge their idea of perfection by revealing that God's character is not based on His anger at people for what they do. Rather, His love for people remains despite what they do.

Jesus' teaching captivated the crowd. He spoke with an authority and wisdom they had never heard. Perhaps more amazing than what He said, however, is who He claimed to be and what He came to do. Different from every other prophet or guru in Israel's history, Jesus referred to Himself as Lord and made claims as sweeping as coming to fulfill the law of Moses (see Matthew 5:17; 7:21).

Up to this point, the news had spread that Jesus was a miracle worker who had sage advice. That much was apparent. But was there anything more to Him that might prove He was something more? People were stunned by what followed.

The Face of God Returns

Most in the crowd who followed Jesus down the mountain seemed content to take a wait-and-see approach to His bold assertions. A man with leprosy, however, lunged forward to find out right away. He needed to know if Jesus was who He claimed to be, and if He loved as He claimed to love. For him, hope was now or never. You see, in those days, leprosy was a shameful disease. Because leprosy was so contagious and painful, a person who suffered with it could not be among uninfected people. The Law dictated that they were unclean, and it relegated them to the outskirts of town, isolated from others. People took this so seriously that if anyone approached a leper, the leper needed to shout "unclean" and ring a bell. Imagine the shame.

For all those reasons, the leper who thrust himself toward Jesus took a huge risk. If Jesus were not the loving Lord that He illustrated, who knows what punishment the man would have received. But he had to take the chance. "A man with leprosy approached him and knelt before him. 'Lord,' the man said, 'if you are willing, you can heal me and make me clean'" (Matthew 8:2). Jesus did not hesitate to respond. Remarkably, to the man's bold request, Jesus reached out and touched him. "'I am willing,' he said. 'Be healed!'" (verse 3). The leprosy dissolved immediately.

Though Jesus was already known for performing miracles, this was the first one described in detail in Matthew's gospel. That is not coincidental. Everything about the encounter details God's goodness in a way that flies in the face of what people had believed about God. Remember that in the years after the Ten Commandments, religious leaders created many laws beyond the original 613. Yes, God's Law did instruct that lepers remain isolated from other people (see Leviticus 13:46). This was to preserve the health of the people. But humans took it further. Still many years from a full revelation of good and evil (and many more years from scientific explanations for disease), people interpreted leprosy as one of God's punishments for sin; therefore, they treated lepers as one of God's enemies.[2]

If God was mad at lepers, Jesus did not show it. His reaction to the man demonstrated quite the opposite. Most obviously, He reached out and touched him. What kind of person would put themselves at risk like that? Jesus, needless to say, was no mere person. This was but one demonstration that He is God in the flesh.

But there is more to this than what modern readers usually see. Back then, God and sinners could not be present together without some sort of buffer. This began in the days of Moses. Speaking through smoke atop Mount Sinai, the Lord warned that people may no longer approach His presence.

The perfect and the imperfect could not mix. The combination would result in death (see Exodus 19:21).

To summarize a long, storied history, after He gave the Law, the Lord hid His face from people. That does not mean He was always against them. In Scripture, one's face is representative of his or her true character.[3]

Hiding His face meant that God stopped relating to people through His essence of pure grace. No doubt, He still showed it from time to time. The Lord assured Moses, "I will show mercy to anyone I choose, and I will show compassion to anyone I choose." And He did. We discussed that in the last chapter. The Lord added, "But you may not look directly at my face" (Exodus 33:19–20). Although God remained present with His people, from that moment forward, they mostly heard Him speak from a distance and saw His radiance behind a cloud. Moses was privileged to see His back. Nobody was to see His face. Until Jesus.

When the leprous man knelt before Jesus, the Lord could have offered mercy without touching him. He could have granted compassion without looking into his eyes. Yet Jesus stooped down to meet the man at his level. In doing so, He proved a god-like immortality and immunity to disease. That is notable. To a people who believed that disease is the product of God's punishment, Jesus' healing expressed both a willingness and ability to forgive sin. That is huge. More marvelously, though, Jesus conveyed that God is here among imperfect people to reconcile them with His face. That is a message that He continued with nearly every subsequent healing. But this was only the beginning. Jesus had much more to say through what He did, especially about what it means that God is love.

What Is Love

I was born in the mid-1980s. I do not remember much from that decade, except for big hair. (Though that could be from the photos of girls that my oldest brother dated.) Most of my memories begin in the early nineties, around kindergarten. For at least the first few years of that decade, some of my most vivid memories are attached to songs. To this day, certain tunes transport me back to summers at our city's public pool, where pop radio played as the backdrop to cannon-ball jumps and the smell of chlorine. For a minute, I see myself there, sprinting toward the pool with no cares other than my feet getting burned by the sun-scorched concrete.

Now that I am old enough to understand them, I have noticed something about those eighties and nineties songs. Many beg to know what love is or what is love (various song titles ask the same question in different ways). From their lyrics, it seems as if the songwriters experienced love in hurtful ways. Yet, despite the pain they faced, they kept the hope that it should be different.

The search to define love, of course, is not limited to songs in the golden age of music—err, I mean, at the end of the twentieth century. "What is love?" may be one of the most human questions to ask. Experiencing love is a driving force of our existence. It was made to be. Sadly, however, as the songs express, many only know love through the lens of a broken system. Most of what people say about it today reflects that. Search for the word *love* in the dictionary, and you will find two popular definitions.[4] The first is "affection based on admiration, benevolence, or common interests."

The second is "attraction based on sexual desire." Both definitions are based upon something; both are conditional.

The world's definitions of love are flawed enough. But many religious definitions are not any better. Some are worse, in my opinion. Since the New Testament revealed that God is love, many Christians have defined and demonstrated love according to how they understand God. Those sign-wavers that I used to encounter on the street corners believe they are acting in love. They might argue that it is loving to warn someone that they are running into a burning building. Most Christians, however, are not so "turn or burn" in their definition. They prefer a mixture of grace and truth. That sounds great, even godly. Except that truth is often confused for law. And love is, therefore, demonstrated through both subtle and not-so-subtle ways of threatening or correcting someone into the faith.

Absolutely, God is love. This means that love looks like Him. But God did not leave that vague and open for interpretation. He went to great lengths to define love clearly. Want to know who God is and what He looks like? Look to Jesus. Through the New Testament, God unveiled that Jesus is His visible image and His true character in the flesh (see Colossians 1:15; Hebrews 1:3). Jesus claimed the same Himself, asserting, "Anyone who has seen me has seen the Father!" (John 14:9).

As we have already explored, Jesus is characterized as "unfailing love" (John 1:14). Since He is love at its purest, we should look to Him to define it. Believe it or not, this brings us back to the nineties. Because it was then that rubber bracelets inscribed with W.W.J.D. went viral. I had one in navy blue and neon green. Do you recall what the letters reminded us to ask ourselves? The answer: What Would Jesus Do? That is a healthy question. More than a few times, I could have avoided some drama had I asked myself that before sending a text. I wish people would ask themselves that before they opine on social media. Nonetheless, the best way to find out what Jesus would do is to look at what He did.

The four gospels were written strategically to show who God is by what Jesus did. And I stress *strategically*. Like any letter today, each gospel was written by its author to convey a message to a specific audience at the time. Since Jesus did far more than what would fit inside of a readable letter, Matthew, Mark, Luke, and John chose to include stories that best made their point to their Jewish and Gentile readers (see John 21:25). As I said earlier, it is not coincidental that Matthew emphasized the healing of the leper at the beginning of Jesus' ministry. This story not only introduced what Jesus came to do, but it set the stage to show an important truth about love: it knows no boundaries.

Love Knows No Boundaries

Have you seen the t-shirt based upon Jesus' Sermon on the Mount? There are various versions of it, but on the front, they all include His words, "Love your neighbor." Printed on the back is a list of kinds of people that some Christians these days consider more enemies than neighbors: Muslim, black, white, Asian, gay, addicted, liberal, and conservative, among others. If we are honest, there is a label on that list that represents someone we struggle to understand, much less love. One equivalent in Jesus' day was a Samaritan.

To understand why Jesus' fellow Jews especially despised Samaritans, you must know a bit of history. In short, Samaritans were descendants of Israelites who had intermarried with other races. In Jewish eyes, they were half-breeds who strayed from the Law and adopted worldly customs. It was their rule, therefore, to avoid Samaritans at all costs and never speak to one. They believed that the Samaritans did not deserve the dignity.

Do you think Jesus followed the rule? Never. Immediately after His baptism, the apostle John described Jesus' first act of defiance. It happened when Jesus had to get to Galilee from Judea. If you look at a Bible map, you will see the conundrum. Samaria is situated between the two regions. Avoiding it would have added days to His trip. He had to go through it (see John 4:4).

While he strolled slowly through Samaria at noontime, the heat made Jesus feel His humanity. Tired and thirsty, He took a break at the community well. Along came a shame-filled Samaritan woman. It was customary to draw water in the cool of the day. This lady snuck to the well alone in the heat to avoid the judgmental glances and whispers of the self-righteous. She had been through five marriages. When she met Jesus, she lived openly unmarried with man number six. In a small village of hundreds, imagine the rumors people spread about her.

As the woman bent down to draw water from the well, Jesus did something unthinkable—uncouth, even, for a Jewish rabbi. He spoke to her. In that single act, He broke at least three rules. Not only did Jews avoid Samaritans, but a Jewish man also shied away from speaking to a woman in public. They surely never involved themselves with someone considered unclean. Jesus shattered these conventions. He spoke to the Samaritan woman. He asked her for a drink, and He then mentioned a gift God had for her. He then introduced Himself as that gift.

There is so much to this story that I do not have the space here to retell.[5] Through His entire interaction, Jesus showed unbridled love to this woman—this Samaritan sinner—by treating her as someone who was as made in God's image as any pure-blood Jew. By asking her for something, He showed her dignity. By mentioning God's gift, He proved her worth. By revealing Himself as her Savior, He demonstrated that nothing counts someone out of the invitation into God's family. (I see a model of evangelism in this progression, but that is a different message.)

Sure, Jesus did not wink at her sin. But He also did not use it to threaten her. Instead, He chose to love her out of shame and let that love do its work from there. It did. The woman left her meeting with Jesus to share His Good News with the very people that she had been afraid to face just minutes earlier. In his gospel, John makes sure to emphasize the result, which would have shocked Jewish readers: many Samaritans found salvation in Him (see verses 39–42).

As you read through the gospels, pay close attention to Jesus' interactions with Samaritans. He not only healed them, but He also used them as examples of good-hearted and merciful people. He referred to them as neighbors (see Luke 10:30–37). Throughout His ministry, Jesus did the same with virtually every other people group that had once been considered far too imperfect for God's affection. Lepers, Samaritans, Gentiles, Roman officers, tax collectors, bleeding women, and blind men—they were all touched by Jesus.

Today, if you ask, "What would Jesus do?" regarding some-one on some contemporary "unclean" list, you will find the answer in what Jesus did. He loved them through His touch, His time, and His invitation. Today, if you ask, "Can God love me?" you will also find the answer in what Jesus did. His actions speak for Him with a resounding, "Yes!" Jesus demonstrated that real love knows no bigotry, it knows no boundaries. Nothing has the power to stop God from loving you (see Romans 8:38). No past regret. No present imperfec-tion. And one more thing that literally killed Him to prove: no rule.

Love Prefers People over Rules

A recent interaction with a local burger joint underscored my "beef" with legalism: it refuses to break the rules to do the right thing. Here is the short of what happened. After waiting thirty minutes for fast food, I asked for a manager to cancel my order. Two more minutes passed, and no one came. I was not feeling impatient, but I had to leave for a meeting. As I walked to my car a bit "hangry," I phoned the restaurant to request a refund. The manager promised to do so. Two weeks later, I noticed that my credit card statement did not reflect his promise. I gave this guy the benefit of the doubt. The restaurant seemed understaffed, and I was sure he had been pulled in another direction before he had the chance to pro-cess the refund. The problem was that when I later called the restaurant to make this right, a manager insisted they could not issue the refund. Apparently, too much time had passed.

"Two weeks is too much time?" I questioned. She said this to the wrong person. As someone who operates an organization that processes credit cards, I know that every system has an easy-to-click refund button for transactions that date back far more than two weeks. That is why I clarified kindly to the manager that the issue was not that they *cannot* refund me, but that they *would not* refund me. She acknowledged this by leaning on some corporate policy. But what is a better policy? Upholding a rule at all costs, or breaking a rule to do the right thing for someone? I suspect this manager upheld the rule out of fear of what her boss might do if she broke it. That is the power of legalism. It manipulates people with fear of being punished by someone above.

The world of Jesus was filled with low- and mid-level managers called Pharisees and Sadducees. Because they feared God's wrath, they went to great lengths to uphold the rules, even if it meant leaving someone to suffer. They believed God preferred the rules. Jesus demonstrated that God prefers people. He killed many of their sacred cows to do so. One was a rule about the Sabbath.

The fourth of the Ten Commandments instructs, "Remember to observe the Sabbath day by keeping it holy" (Exodus 20:8). The Bible goes on to say that no work may be done on this day (see verses 9–11). The religious leaders believed that work included helping people. Jesus dared to question their logic. He contended that God made Sabbath to meet people's needs, not the other way around (see Mark 2:27). He then demonstrated that point by healing a man on the Sabbath, right in front of religious leaders. Though He did not exert any more effort than to say to the man, "Hold out your hand," the Pharisees were appalled. Breaking this rule was the rebellion they needed to see to put Him to death (see Matthew 12:9–14). What they could not have imagined, however, was that the very means that they used to kill Him—the cross—brought their system's greatest undoing.

With the institution of the Law, God held people accountable for sin. Since justice is one of God's qualities, it is well within His rights to enforce punishment and reparation for sin. And He did for thousands of years through wrath and sacrifices. He didn't have to change this. But He wanted to. By taking on human flesh as Jesus, God chose to show that mercy is more important to Him than sacrifice (see Matthew 9:13).

On the cross, God chose to satisfy His Law and justice all by Himself, once and for all (see Hebrews 9:28). Jesus became the Lamb of God to forgive the sin of the world, just as His cousin John had prophesied. This reconciled and put humanity permanently at peace with God, just as the angels announced at His birth. The cross was God's ultimate act to define unfailing love. He chose forgiveness, establishing that people are even more important than His own rules. And from it, He gave something more to help us see and relate to Him, ourselves, and others without the lens of sin. Let's continue in the next chapter.

QUESTIONS FOR PERSONAL REFLECTION

1. What feelings or images have you associated with the word *holy*? Where did these originate? How would you describe God's holiness now?

2. What is your favorite story about Jesus from the gospels? How does what you learned in this chapter enrich it?

3. What are the differences between Jesus' demonstrations of love and what you have experienced from people?

4. Think about some kinds of people that you do not understand. Based on what Jesus did, how do you think He would interact with them today?

5. Reflect upon the truth that "God prefers people over rules." How might this affect your relationship with God, yourself, and others?

5

The God Who Is on Your Side

> "But when the Father sends the Advocate as my representative . . . he will teach you everything and will remind you of everything I have told you." —John 14:26

Along my route home from the grocery store, I felt the temptation to speed up before the approaching traffic light turned from yellow to red. Since I am sure that it is one of the longest traffic lights on earth, I could have saved myself some real time. This time, however, I chose to play it safe. I let off the gas and braked gently so that the grocery bag of milk and eggs on my passenger seat did not fly toward the floorboard. It worked. A few seconds before the light changed, I came to a smooth, complete stop, leaving enough space between the crosswalk and me.

After only ten seconds, the hood of an all-white SUV greeted me in my rearview mirror. I suddenly was glad that

I had not accepted my personal dare to beat the light. The black push bar attached to the vehicle's grill told me that this was not just another citizen behind me. That hunch was even more confirmed when I glanced up to see the "cherries" (the lights on top of the car), as we called them in the nineties. Thankfully, they were not flashing.

While at the traffic light that seemed would never change, I continued to glance in my mirror. For at least five minutes, the officer typed on his computer, then spoke into his shoulder walkie-talkie, then typed some more. Though I wondered what he was doing, I was not too worried that it had anything to do with me. After all, I was not speeding, texting, nor had I run that light.

Finally, when the light turned green, I eased myself across the intersection, then set my cruise control to match the speed limit. With my hands on the wheel at ten and two, despite my efforts to model perfection, the officer continued to follow me closely. When I turned, he turned, again and again and again. This went on for another five minutes—which feels like an eternity when an officer tailgates you.

As he continued to follow, I grew insecure in my ability to drive. My heart rate increased, and my mind raced about what could be wrong. I went through a mental checklist of possibilities. *Is my license plate tag expired? Is a brake light out? Is there an unpaid toll on my record?* I figured that I was safe on the first two. I remembered affixing the new sticker to my plate just a month earlier. And since my car was barely more than a year old, I was confident that my brake lights were all right. An unpaid toll, though? Well, that could be a viable issue here in Central Florida, land of the toll roads. Fortunately, at an intersection about a half mile from my house, the officer and I parted ways. I continued straight; he went right. My heart rate returned to normal, and my mind was put back at ease.

I do not know the officer's intentions, of course. Perhaps his route to wherever he went was 90 percent the same as mine. Whatever the case, as I reflected on what had just happened, like a good preacher, I gleaned a few lessons. First, the constant scrutiny (even if it was only in my mind) was counterproductive to safe driving. The pressure of keeping the right speed and distance between cars while maintaining all the other nuances of driving weakened my physical senses. My heart rate alone was enough to keep me from thinking clearly.

Second, I realized that I had been more concerned with what I could be doing wrong than with the road and other drivers. If this had continued, it is inevitable that I would have made a mistake. Lastly, I recognized that the presence of this officer is exactly how many people envision God's presence in their lives. They see Him as a cosmic sin police, waiting to catch and correct their every mistake. This is sad because that contradicts everything that Jesus said and did.

God and Sinners Reconciled

Crucifixion day seemed a world away from when people greeted Jesus with palm branches or sat to listen to Him for hours. Most in the crowd around the cross considered Jesus in good company, dangling between two rebels. In a short time, religious leaders successfully made the case for why He posed such a threat and should be killed in the cruelest way known to humankind. Nobody protested as soldiers spat on and beat Him with rods, whipped Him with ropes of shrapnel, and pressed a wreath of inch-long thorns into His forehead. People shouted slurs as spikes sliced through His hands and feet.

When you think about all the cruelty that Jesus suffered on that day, be mindful that He did not endure any of it accidentally. Jesus knew the fate that He would face before He came to earth. In order to satisfy God's justice and forgive sin once and for all, He willingly offered Himself to be filleted like a sacrificial lamb (see Hebrews 10:5–7). He chose to be there, dying for those who put Him there. No greater act of love has ever been witnessed in history.

After a bloody and nearly suffocating six hours on the cross, Jesus mustered up the strength and breath for one final declaration. "It is finished" (John 19:30). He announced this from atop the tree, confirming that His mission was accomplished. If people had any questions as to what that mission was, what happened next provided the answer. The moment that Jesus died, "the curtain in the sanctuary of the Temple was torn in two, from top to bottom" (Matthew 27:51).

While modern readers might miss the significance of the torn curtain, the Jewish people would not have. For many years, the temple had been the location where sacrifices were carried out faithfully according to the Law of Moses. In the temple, a curtain separated God's presence from the people. It was a constant reminder that sin separates God and humans. Once per year, a high priest was permitted to cross the curtain to make atonement for that sin.

This all changed on crucifixion day. Through Jesus' sacrifice, God and sinners—the Perfect and the imperfect—were reconciled and put at peace with each other. The torn temple curtain was a profound symbol of that. Though crucifixion day was not what Jesus' followers had envisioned as the fate of the Messiah, they should not have been surprised. He spoke to them frequently about His departure. Yet it seems that His words fell on deaf ears.

I suppose that is understandable. Over the course of His short, three-year ministry, Jesus provided plenty of questions to occupy their minds. The kinds of people that He helped, healed, touched, and talked to were perplexing enough. The idea that God could live among sinners was revolutionary for them to consider, if not flirting with blasphemy. Jesus giving Himself up to be killed, though, was inconceivable. As was His claim that it would benefit everyone for Him to do so.

The Promise of Something Better

After about fifteen years of military service, a friend of mine started to consider leaving the military. I understood his reason; he no longer wanted to live under the threat of being deployed away from his wife and kids for months at a time. But since all his employment offers were from companies out of the state, leaving his job meant that he and his family would have to leave me. Within only a few years, we all had grown very close. I often joined them for dinner in the evenings, and I sometimes tagged along on their vacations. I feared what life would be like if they moved away.

Since I did not want to entertain the idea that my friends might not be near me anymore, I did my best to ignore any discussion about it. When I could not ignore it, I resorted to some of my best spiritual manipulation tactics. Things that sounded like, "God said . . ." or "God told me. . . ." Once, as a joke, I attempted to program my friend's phone to say, "Holy Ghost" when I texted him. My goal was to make it look like God had texted, "Don't move." But I made a typo in the process. My text came from the "Holy Goat," instead. The joke was on me!

As I said, Jesus gave His followers plenty of warning about His death. He even predicted the way He would die. One of the reasons they could hardly grasp the thought was because they did not want to think about it. As I did when my friend mused about moving, Jesus' disciples either grew quiet or reprimanded Him for such talk (see Mark 8:31–32). Life with Jesus was strange, yes. It had its confusing moments, sure. But it was also thrilling and promising. Who would want to go back to the way things had been?

Jesus, however, never implied that things would return to the way things had been. Not even close. Adding to their bewilderment, He promised that they would benefit greatly from His departure because God would send a helper, the Holy Spirit (see John 14:16; 16:7). To be sure, this was not entirely foreign to them. The Jewish people understood the concept of God's Spirit being with people.

In Israel's history, God's Spirit had rested upon judges, prophets, and certain warriors, giving them supernatural power to accomplish His purposes. People anticipated a time that had been prophesied about when God would pour out His Spirit on all people (see Joel 2:28). But God's Spirit *on* someone is all they expected or could comprehend. Jesus promised something different. He said the Spirit would not only rest on people temporarily but would live inside of and remain with anyone who believed—*anyone*. What is more,

Jesus described God's Spirit in a way that they had never heard. He called Him "the Advocate as my representative" (John 14:26).

Pause for a minute to consider the word *advocate*. What comes to mind? Do you think of someone campaigning for a cause? Or someone standing up for what is right? Today's textbook definitions only scratch the surface of what Jesus meant when He used the word, which is *paraclete* in Greek. In the English New Testament, *paraclete* is not only translated as "advocate," but also as "helper" and "counselor."[1]

These days when you hear these words, it is tempting to imagine a therapist. I long pictured the Holy Spirit more like a sober-faced, straight-talking psychologist who listens to my complaints and then advises me on what to do or not do. Undoubtedly, God listens, and He advises. But this therapist concept is modern. There were no mental health counselors in Bible times. Back then, a *paraclete* was legal counsel. It was the title given to an attorney who stood ready to defend their clients against accusations of wrongdoing.[2]

Our contemporary concept of a defense attorney offers tremendous insight into what Jesus meant when He promised an Advocate. Fortunately, I have no experience with a defense attorney, but I know people who do. And I have seen them played on television many times. Though attorneys may know incriminating facts about their clients, they will never bring those facts up. Attorneys will never offer evidence that supports any accusations or charges against their clients. The defense attorney's sole responsibility is to plead the client's innocence. Attorneys are always on the side of their clients.

When Jesus revealed, "the Father [will send] the Advocate as my representative," He meant that God's Spirit will remain alongside and inside of believers to prove their innocence. Furthermore, He will do it in a way that represents Jesus. As a customer service representative is an extension of a company's voice and character, the Holy Spirit is an extension of Jesus' character. This is why Jesus assured it is better for Him to depart. In the flesh, He was limited to one place at one time. In the Spirit, He can be everywhere at all times.

Last chapter we explored a few examples of Jesus' interactions with people. These make up only a small sample of how the gospels consistently describe Him. He never condemned, shamed, nor belittled any struggler. Sure, He was firm at times, but only as He confronted the follies of legalists and the scams of religious opportunists. With everyone else, however, He never acted as the "sin police," waiting to catch them in a mistake. Far from it! Jesus went out of His way to touch the untouchables, speak to the unspeakables, and forgive the unforgivable. He offered the fallen, the broken, and the burdened a hand up and a way out. The Bible encapsulates His time on earth like this: "Jesus went around doing good and healing all who were oppressed by the devil, for God was with him" (Acts 10:38).

Shortly after Jesus' ascension to heaven, the Holy Spirit came down as He promised. The book of Acts tells the surprising stories of how people from every nation, tribe, and tongue received the Spirit. And He has never left. Today, He continues to swirl around all of us and make His home inside of every believer. Yes, the Holy Spirit is with us now, as Jesus was then, amid chaos, turbulence, and imperfection—as our Advocate. Though we still might not understand everything He does, one thing is certain: advocates help people, they do not beat them up.

The Real Role of the Holy Spirit

On social media, I once shared the last part of that sentence—that advocates do not beat people up—as an illustration. It was yet another time that people showed me their *buts*. I was surprised at how polarizing this idea is. What I meant as pithy encouragement turned into a theological firestorm in the comments below the post. The criticisms all sounded similar—something like, "But He hates sin!" or "But He disciplines us!" I learned that the thinking of many Christians is so warped by religion that they do not feel right unless they feel wrong.

Undeniably, the Holy Spirit addresses sin, but not in the ways that most people think. As Jesus' representative, the Spirit addresses sin as He did, which is to offer Himself as the answer to it. This is His primary role, which He does for both unbelievers and believers, just in different ways.

The Holy Spirit's Role on Unbelievers

With His promise to the disciples about the coming of the Advocate, Jesus added, "When he comes, he will convict the world of its sin, and of God's righteousness, and of the coming judgement" (John 16:8). The angry, street-corner sign-wavers love this line. They think they advocate for the Advocate by naming in black marker the sins from which people are to turn—or else. But Jesus had more to say on the subject. In His next breath, He named the sin. And it was just one. "The world's sin is that it refuses to believe in me" (verse 9).

Rather than specific sins, Jesus described that unbelief is what the Holy Spirit addresses with those in the world. Yet again, the reason comes back to John the Baptist's prophecy about what Jesus would accomplish on the cross. Recall that at Jesus' baptism, John declared, "Behold, the Lamb of God, who takes away the sin of the world" (John 1:29 ESV). On the cross, Jesus declared it finished (see John 19:30). The apostle Paul explained that this was the moment that God stopped counting people's sins against them (see 2 Corinthians 5:19).

Part of the wonder and Good News of what Jesus accomplished is that individual sins no longer separate God and people. Remember the point of the torn curtain? Accordingly, the Holy Spirit is not concerned with naming or managing individual sins. If stopping sin is a prerequisite for salvation, we would all remain hopeless. Since God knows that is impossible for humans, He sent Jesus to end the problem of sin for us. Belief in Jesus and what He did—not the absence of sin—is what secures someone's salvation and eternal destiny with God (see John 3:16; Romans 3:25). The Holy Spirit works consistently on unbelievers to show them that. And He does it in the same way that Jesus did while on earth, which is through unfailing love.

God often uses believers to help reveal the message of Jesus to the world. To me, there is no greater privilege in life; however, for at least the first decade of my faith, I thought my part was to help people live worthy of the message. This only left me intensely frustrated because people continued to fall short. What I could not acknowledge at the time was that I fell short as well. The beginning of the end of what I call my "holiness police" years came when I sought the Lord's advice for how to minister to some guys at my local gym. I begged Him for a strategy to help them stop what I believed was a grave sin in their lives. God broke through my self-righteous "burden" with a single suggestion. *Instead of looking for what the devil might be doing in their lives, look for what I am doing, and then come alongside of that.*

God's instruction to me that day was a paradigm shift. At the time, I had not considered that the Holy Spirit works 24/7 on unbelievers to woo them to Him in ways that I cannot detect. I should have, though, because it is what Jesus promised. Like Jesus did with the Samaritan woman, God's Spirit meets each unbeliever where they are. And not with a sign that says, "turn or burn." He comes with signs that affirm *I made you, I love you, and I want you in My family forever.* Sometimes those signs are words. Sometimes they are actions. Sometimes they are miracles. Regardless of how they appear, the apostle Paul instructed that God draws people to Himself through kindness (see Romans 2:4).

Learn the lesson that I did with my friend who was on the verge of moving. When you attempt to speak for the Holy Spirit with "don'ts" or threats, you only end up proving yourself to be more like a "holy goat." You will expend a lot of energy but get nowhere. Remember that as their Creator, God knows what people need better than you do. And God cares about them far more than you ever could. Let yourself off the hook regarding having to "fix" them. Simply allow God's love to speak through you. Often, that sounds as plain as, "God loves you." Your confirmation of that is sure to complement the way that He is already at work in their lives.

The Holy Spirit's Role in Believers

Most Christians would agree in theory that God's love is the most effective agent for change, not only for unbelievers, but also for believers. What we do and say, however, does not often agree. Many Christians and churches take great pride in how they love "sinners." And to be fair, many really do love them well and as unconditionally as humanly possible. Yet I have noticed that this version of love tends to end as soon as someone says yes to Jesus. At this point, it is as if we believe that, as Jesus turned water into wine, He supernaturally transforms love from "unconditional" to "tough." Some believe that while there are no requirements to obtain salvation, there are 1,001 requirements to maintain it. "Do not worry," we say while we send the new believer on his or her way. "You have the Holy Spirit to help you live up to what God expects."

Please forgive me if what I just said sounds cynical. The Holy Spirit who lives inside of us provides strength, of course. Yes, He helps us in our weakness (see Romans 8:26). He is so good like that. But why do many Christians in whom the Holy Spirit dwells still live stressed and frustrated and question their salvation? It is because they feel they do not meet the expectations placed upon them. Some fear there is something wrong with them. Others fear there is something wrong with God. The truth, however, has nothing to do with anything that they or God lack. The Holy Spirit does not help believers meet God's expectations. But rather, as the Advocate, He reminds believers that Jesus met God's expectations for them.

As a believer, the Holy Spirit will never argue that you disappointed or failed God. He will never threaten punishment or provoke fear of God's retaliation. Like a defense attorney, the Holy Spirit is there to offer evidence of your innocence, which He does not have to hunt to find. He does not rest His case upon how much money you gave to the church, how many Scripture verses you have memorized, or if you cried enough tears to prove your sorrow. No, when it comes to your standing with God because of any past or present sin, the Holy Spirit rests His case on Jesus, who did all the work necessary to forgive you and make you right.

When Jesus spoke to His disciples about the Advocate, He revealed what He sounds like, which is Him. Jesus promised, "He will teach you everything and will remind you of everything I have told you" (John 14:26). This was to help ensure that the disciples did not slip gradually back into the old way of works-based faith. Having lived years with their minds programmed to the Law, that threat was very real. Consequently, the Holy Spirit renewed them continually with the words of Jesus. It seems He kept the love part of His Sermon on the Mount afresh in their minds. Scholars have discovered that "love your enemies" was the most cited and shared verse in the first few centuries of Christianity.[3] The Holy Spirit especially reminded them of the cross and taught them about its far-reaching personal and cultural implications. With the Spirit-empowered message and demonstrations of God's love for everyone, Christianity grew by 4 million percent by the year 300.[4]

The Holy Spirit continues to work and speak the same in the lives of believers today. He is the voice of Jesus and His revelation given to the New Testament writers. To defend you from the fear of punishment, He might sound like Jesus' declaration on the cross, "It is finished." To protect you from shame and striving, He might sound like His words through the apostle Paul, "So we are made right with God through faith and not by obeying the law" (Romans 3:28). Certainly, when you fall, the Holy Spirit will uplift and empower you with "God loves you."

"But God disciplines those He loves!" some argue. And there is no doubt that Scripture explicitly says this (see Hebrews 12:6). But it does not say "condemns," "criticizes," or "afflicts." Unfortunately, in the same way that experience distorts the definition of love for many people, it also distorts what is meant by "discipline." Perhaps you read that word and wince because it brings back to you the sound of your father's belt clearing his belt loops. Or a verbal beat down from your mama. Or the teacher who called on you to solve the math problem on the chalkboard because he knew you did not know how. But the Greek word used for discipline, *paideuō*, was never intended to provoke fear in people, because it is not about punishment. It means to "train or educate."[5]

Concluding His promise of the Advocate, Jesus tells His disciples that He will guide them into all truth and tell them about the future (see John 16:13–14). In other words, the Holy Spirit will train and educate. In this role, think of the Holy Spirit like a mentor, not a drill sergeant. Mentors are invited intimately into the lives of people to help them navigate the present and the future. From the benefit of experience and objectivity, mentors offer suggestions. They offer words of caution and course correction, too. I am grateful for the presence of numerous mentors in my life, even though their advice stings at times. My pride can get temporarily hurt when a mentor reveals something that I did not notice. But there is no shame because I know that he or she has my best interest in mind.

The Holy Spirit is your greatest, most trustworthy mentor because He knows you and your future completely. He knows what makes you the most effective and what steals your strength. He sees what is coming against you and will guide and empower you to make whatever adjustments will help you avoid danger and ensure success. Sure, His voice might sound challenging at times, but it is never condemning, belittling, mocking, or frustrated. Nor does it insist that you must earn anything—not love, not forgiveness, not trust, not promises. If there is something that God wants you to do or somewhere He desires you to go, He will love you to it while He walks you through it.

Keep in mind that there is nothing about you that God does not already know. Yet, despite knowing everything that you did do and will do, He is with you and promises to remain with you. You cannot scare God away. As your Advocate, the Holy Spirit is on your side, at your side, and inside of you to defend, encourage, empower, teach, and guide. Do you sense Him in this moment? It is okay if you do not. Feelings are not the definitive indicator of God's presence. But if you fear that you never sense His presence, there could be something in the way. The next chapter will explain.

QUESTIONS FOR PERSONAL REFLECTION

1. How has your view of the Holy Spirit and His role in the lives of unbelievers and believers changed after reading this chapter?

2. Reflect upon Jesus' declaration, "It is finished!" Since discovering its meaning, what are some questions, fears, or feelings in you that should end?

3. Can you remember a time when you played the role of the Holy Spirit in someone else's life? What was the result?

4. Consider some of the "voices" you have heard internally and externally. In what ways do they represent the Advocate or the Accuser?

5. As your Advocate, the Holy Spirit defends you with truth. What truths or Scripture verses come to mind that testify to Jesus' work in your life?

6

The Key to Intimacy

> Once you were far away from God, but now you have been brought near to him through the blood of Christ. —Ephesians 2:13

I became frantic one day when I could not find my phone. While, admittedly, I spend too much time on it, my anxiety was not from detoxing for an hour. First, losing something like my phone is out of character for me. I never leave my house without patting my pockets to make a mental checklist of *keys, wallet, cell phone.* My primary phone was in my hands, though. I lost the phone I had just sold online for hundreds of dollars that I needed to deliver to the buyer that day.

In case you forgot, I am a tech enthusiast. My ministry also offers a mobile app, which means it is important that I have the latest devices and platforms for testing. Each year, I upgrade to a new phone and largely pay for it by what I make from selling my old one. These days, I usually ship to buyers from an online marketplace. Back then, I preferred to avoid some fees and deliver the phone to a local buyer personally.

In this case, after a couple weeks of dealing with scams and people who ghosted me, I finally had a real buyer who was willing to meet at a public parking lot. But two hours before our meeting, my phone was missing.

I was at an office a few miles from my house when I noticed it was gone. *That's strange*, I thought at first. *I know that I had the phone in my hands when I left this morning.* I figured it was on my kitchen table, so I drove the few miles back home to get it. But it was not there. After I searched every room in the house with no success, I convinced myself that it must really be at the office.

That is when three words popped into my mind: *Check the trash.* I dismissed them. *There is no way that I threw the phone in the trash!* I assured myself. I drove back to the office, certain that I would find it hidden in a nook that I had overlooked. But after combing the office high and low, I did not find the phone.

As the meeting with the buyer drew nearer, I grew more frantic. And the more insistent that voice in my head became, too. *Check-the-trash,* I heard again and again, gently but also determinedly. I was as determined, though—that I had not thrown that phone away! Still, desperation moved me to drive home one last time. After I parked my car in the driveway, I headed reluctantly to the garbage bin at the curb. When I lifted the lid, atop several trash bags that reeked of food spoiling in the Florida heat, there was the Best Buy bag that contained the phone.

With the benefit of hindsight, I pieced together what had happened. It was trash day. And like every trash day, I took the bin to the curb just before leaving for the office. This time, however, I also held the bag that contained the phone.

At some point, I got distracted and placed the bag inside the garbage bin and went on my way.

Less than an hour from meeting the buyer, I felt a huge sense of relief for having found it there. I took the bag inside and spritzed it with cologne so that it did not smell like trash. Then, I drove away. Not ten seconds later, I heard the beep-beep-beep of the garbage truck entering my subdivision. I thanked God when I realized that I found the phone less than thirty minutes before it would have been gone forever.

Some will chalk the "voice" I heard up to my subconscious or paranoia. For a while, I did, too. But when I saw that garbage truck, I recognized there was far more to it than anything my mind had concocted on its own. The timing alone demonstrates a precision that could not have come from me. A few minutes extra here or there and I would have been out at least a few hundred dollars. I am convinced that the words I heard came from the presence of God within me. Not just because I want to believe that. But because it is exactly what Scripture affirms that God does.

How God Makes His Presence Known

Growing up in the religious tradition that I did, I hardly knew that God was personal. Occasionally, I read about someone in history who had a dream or a vision. But I had never heard a contemporary of mine who claimed that God spoke to them. That changed quickly when, as a teenager, I attended a charismatic church. At that church, hearing God seemed to be the norm, not the exception. It was common for people's sentences to begin with "God said . . ." or "God told me. . . ." I was in awe. It was as if they had a direct line to God.

In less than a few months, I realized that the people did have a direct line to God, as does everyone—although maybe not as sensationally as I thought at first. Most did not hear an audible voice. Not that it is impossible to hear God audibly. But most heard God as I did on that trash day. They received thoughts or feelings that either aligned with God's Word or His character. I am not naïve, of course. Some of what people considered God was probably themselves. That is true for all of us. No human discerns the Holy Spirit perfectly all the time (see 1 Corinthians 13:9). Still, that does not change the truth that because God is with us, people can and do sense His presence in various ways.

God created humans to have a close and experiential relationship with Him. In the beginning, He spoke with Adam and Eve and walked among them (see Genesis 3:8). Even after sin ran amok, He promised to remain with His people in spirit. He assured Jacob, "I am with you" (Genesis 28:15). He guaranteed Israel that He would never fail nor abandon them (see Deuteronomy 31:6). He led His people from behind a cloud or spoke to them through smoke, fire, dreams, or visions. They sensed Him inside of a tabernacle.

Jesus changed this in a big way. In addition to ending the need for a buffer between God and people, He also promised that people would literally house God's Spirit. Parents, could you house your children and never notice that they are there? Of course not. Not even when they are glued to their smartphones. What purpose would it serve for God to fill us and then go dormant? I cannot think of one.

Certainly, Jesus never implied this. To lead and guide believers, He promised that the Holy Spirit would talk (see John 16:13–15). Like I said, His voice is rarely heard audibly.

Mostly, God speaks through the voice of Scripture, the voices and actions of others, by imparting a random thought into your mind, or by surfacing an indescribable sense to "look there," "trust this," or "remember that."

My faith journey thus far has given me a great deal of insight into how God makes His presence known to people. Better than that, though, I have learned to recognize His voice and presence in my life. I am still learning, obviously. Moments like that trash day happen more often than I care to admit. The process of understanding how God communicates is a constant adventure, just as in any human relationship. Even after knowing Him for decades, you will find nuances and niceties to His voice.

You will also misread and misunderstand Him at times. That is okay. Unlike your spouse, He will not scold you for doing so. Also, unlike a human, God never needs His own space. He does not punish with silence. He never stops listening, not even for a moment. God does not get farther away as a reaction to your actions. Nor does He get closer in response to your devotion. That is something that took me more than a decade to learn. Maybe hearing this takes you by surprise right now. But I ask: how can an omnipresent God who is always with you and in you get any closer to you?

The Myth of the Great God-Blocker

Until I learned what I am about to share, my relationship with God was like riding a rollercoaster. There were "top hat" moments when I felt I had ascended to a height that was next to God. In these times, revelation leapt off the pages of my Bible during devotions. My mind remained focused during prayer and my heart was passionate in worship. Like a coaster, those feelings came quickly, and then plunged just as quickly, sometimes with a barrel roll in between. In the dips, God felt distant and unresponsive, even uninterested. Devotions were dry, as if I had squeezed every bit of life out of Scripture a long time ago. Mostly, I went through the motions, waiting for the upturn. I know that you can relate.

It is not that I do not feel God more on some days than others. Trust me, I do. Feelings are fickle like that. Many factors affect them, including sleep, diet, and the weather. That never changes, which is why you cannot rely upon feelings to measure anything accurately. Reflecting on my feelings of God's presence for years, I especially recognize a factor that is part nature and part nurture. God felt closer when I believed I was a success. He felt distant when I believed I was a disappointment. In my mind, being a success or a disappointment had everything to do with how much of a grip I thought I had on sin.

This factor was influenced by numerous things that go back as far as I can remember. That is why I said it is a mix of nature and nurture. The notion that approval and favor are linked to behavior is part of the shame-nature passed down to us from Adam. Nobody has to teach us this, but then they do. At first, culture reinforces what we feel instinctively. In our environments, we see demonstration after demonstration that good behavior gets rewarded with someone's pleasure and presence. Likewise, bad behavior often results in someone's anger and abandonment. If that is not enough, we are later explicitly told this by religion.

At various times over the years, I heard that sin—even traces of it—is the great God-blocker. I suppose that was baked into me through my childhood tradition. It was echoed, though, in many of the services I attended and the books I read in my twenties. "Your sin separates you from God!" pastors warned in their preaching. I remember one author who argued that to be close to God you have to get all the sin out. His regimen to do so included more prayer, more fasting, more blood, sweat, and tears. I lapped it up, which left me feeling up and down.

When it comes to those who taught this, I believe their intentions were good. As were mine when I used to teach it. I would say the same is true for most teachers. We are all fallen heads instructing fallen heads. Besides, there are Bible verses to back the teaching. That is probably why it passes the smell test for most people. The prophet Isaiah warned, "It's your sins that have cut you off from God." Not only from His presence, but also from His ears. Isaiah added, "Because of your sins, he has turned away and will not listen anymore" (Isaiah 59:2). To me, nothing sounds more dire than losing connection with God to the point that He stops listening. If this is true, then we are right to sound the alarm as loudly as we can.

Thankfully, this is not true. It *was* true. But it is not true anymore. What changed? First, the audience. Israel received this word of caution at a time when they felt that God had abandoned them. Yes, their sin created a real chasm between God and themselves. We explored the reasons why in the previous chapters.

But Isaiah's prophecy did not end with such hopelessness. You must keep reading. Just a handful of verses later, his prophecy assured that separation is not what God desires. Isaiah revealed that God would step in to solve the sin problem Himself. "The Redeemer will come to Jerusalem to buy back those in Israel who have turned from their sins" (verse 20). The result, Isaiah boasted, will be a new covenant in which "[God's] Spirit will not leave them" (verse 21).

Sadly, people mistakenly use Isaiah's prophecy as the proof that sin continues to repel God's Spirit today. When in truth, the prophecy points to Jesus as God's permanent solution for sin. Having said this, I do not mean to imply that sin does not have natural consequences. It does. We see these all around us. But today, separation from God or punishment by Him is not one of them. Any teaching that suggests this not only misses the hope of Old Testament prophecy, but worse, it discounts the cross, the torn curtain, the presence of the Holy Spirit, and the promise of God's new covenant completely.

The Benefits of a New Covenant

The early Church faced a growing problem, especially with the passing of time since Jesus' ascension. It was not persecution. It was not licentious lifestyles. It was that teachers mixed God's Word before Jesus with His Word after Him. The apostle Paul warned that such a mixed message neutralizes Jesus' sacrifice to be of no benefit to people (see Galatians 5:2).

If anything comes between God and people, it is the result of this kind of a message. That is because, as Paul contended, it puts people back in bondage to fear, which is opposite of the Holy Spirit's purpose (see Romans 8:15). To curb the damaging effects of mixture, Paul stressed to his protégé Timothy to "rightly [divide] the word of truth" (2 Timothy 2:15 KJV).

Sadly, some two thousand years later, things are not any better. Paul's instruction is as necessary today as it was back then.

As you know, Scripture is divided into two main parts: the Old Testament and the New Testament. Broadly speaking, these reflect the covenants between God and people. As with contracts today, covenants are agreements between two parties. The old covenant, which was established through Moses, was one of law. In it, humanity's good standing with God depended upon people keeping laws and making sacrifices. The new covenant, which was established through Jesus, is one of grace. In it, humanity's good standing with God depends upon Jesus' sacrifice.

This is called grace because it is not contingent upon human effort. It is a gift received by anyone who believes in who Jesus is and what He accomplished (see Romans 3:22; Ephesians 2:8–9). Think of belief like your signature on a contract that is pre-signed by God in His own blood. There is no ink more permanent.

I, for one, am grateful to live in the covenant of grace. It is enough for me not to have to sacrifice animals. But that is hardly the half of it. The author of Hebrews described it as "a far better covenant with God, based on better promises" (Hebrews 8:6). The benefits are enormous. Consider just a few of them: forgiveness with no strings attached (see Ephesians 1:7), righteousness without requirements (see 2 Corinthians 5:21), and automatic, perpetual peace with God (see Romans 5:1). All of this culminates in a watershed benefit that deserves special attention, especially as it relates to God's presence: "Once you were far away from God, but now you have been brought near to him through the blood of Christ" (Ephesians 2:13).

Meditate for a moment on everything that I just listed: forgiveness, righteousness, peace, and the presence of God—all with no effort. That summarizes the new covenant in which we live. From a human perspective, a covenant like this seems one-sided, to the benefit of people. I suspect that is why the Gospel was such a stumbling block to those living at the time of Jesus. Many feared it was a human concoction to get something for nothing. Jesus went to great lengths to prove otherwise. His signs, wonders, and miracles were part of that. Even after literally seeing how good God is, though, people still believed His message was too good to be true. So they mixed law and grace.

As I said, not much has changed since then. Many still grapple with the idea that a covenant of pure grace is too good to be true. They add disclaimers, qualifiers, *ifs*, and *buts* to the benefits. Thankfully, God still confirms His Good News with signs that validate it (see Mark 16:20). Healings and deliverances continue in ways that no human could ever produce. The Greek word that the apostles used for these is *charisma*, which means "a gift of divine grace."[1] These miracles also continue to flow through exceptionally imperfect people.

Some scratch their heads as to how God works through "dirty hands." Excuses abound, yet everything that God did and does points to a simple answer. It's grace. God divided His Word to point to grace. The Law and the prophets point forward to it. The New Testament letters point back to it. Today, the words and work of the Holy Spirit continue to testify to it. Look around and see—anything that God does for us is not because of our perfection, but despite imperfection. This is the incredible outcome of our reconciliation. It is life in the covenant of grace. And it is why how close or how distant you feel to God is all in your mind.

Closeness Is in Your Mind

In my elementary years, I stole a toy from my neighbor's house. I don't remember what it was. I only remember slipping the thing into my pocket when my neighbors left the room for a minute. As soon as I secured it, I yelled some reason as to why I had to quickly go. It was my only opportunity to escape with the toy. My next challenge was to get it into my house under the radar of my parents, which I did. And I kept it in secret from everyone for a whole agonizing week.

The reason that the week was agonizing was because I had to be around my neighbor's parents. Since we all went to the same school, our parents had worked out a carpooling deal. At 7:15 every school day morning, I walked the short distance to their house, then waited inside until it was time to leave. While the toy remained stolen, I could not shake the feeling that they knew the bad thing that I had done and hated me for it. Consequently, our relationship was affected for a time. I did not speak to them unless they spoke to me first. When they did, my responses were short. I refused to look them in the eyes. Still, except for when I might have faked a stomachache, I saw them every day. Our proximity never changed. They never changed. The only thing that changed was how I acted around them because of how I feared they saw me. That persisted for a while after I secretly returned the toy. Nobody ever found out—until now.

What I experienced is shame. Its effect on relationships is a tale as old as time. Shame is what drove Adam and Eve to hide from God. Because of their wrongdoing, they feared how God saw them. But God was not angry. Remember that He pursued them, then spoke with them, then provided coverings so that they would not feel shame. All they had to do was receive the coverings. The Garden foreshadowed what God would later provide all by Himself through Jesus, which is everything necessary for us to draw near to God and for God to draw near to us.

Do you recognize what I just said? It is one of the most quoted verses in the New Testament. It may have been looming in your mind throughout this chapter. The apostle James encouraged to "Come close to God, and God will come close to you" (James 4:8). But if God is in us and will not leave us, then what should we make of this? As always, context is key. It suggests that this invitation was written to doubters, not believers. You see, James began his letter by greeting Jews who lived outside of Jerusalem (see James 1:1). Many of these were new followers of Jesus, yes, but some were people who waffled between Jesus and Judaism (see v. 8). Others were total unbelievers.

James' encouragement to "come close to God" was an evangelistic appeal to those still on the fence about their faith. What he said next substantiates this idea further. "Wash your hands, you sinners; purify your hearts, for your loyalty is divided between God and the world" (James 4:7). Throughout his letter, James never referred to believers as sinners. And undoubtedly, he knew that God's Spirit lives inside of Christians.

Though James was not addressing believers in this instance, we can glean something from it relating to intimacy with God. After all, as we know from human relationships, intimacy and physical closeness are two very different things. Ever been around a couple on the verge of a bitter divorce? They may be next to each other. They may even speak or look at each other. But they do not really see or hear the other. They are distant because their feelings and emotions have gotten in the way of intimacy.

Of course, God's emotions, thoughts, and feelings about us do not change. Any issue with intimacy is not on His end. It is on our end, influenced by our thoughts. James prefaced his invitation to "come close to God" with this: "So humble yourselves before God. Resist the devil, and he will flee from you" (verse 7). Two words in this verse are especially revealing. First, *humility* is not a negative view of yourself. It means, "having an accurate estimate of one's worth."[2] The Gospel provides this estimate. It is this: God loves you so much that He went to the greatest lengths to send Jesus to provide you permanent peace with Him. That is the measure of your worth, and it could not be higher.

In a human relationship, nothing erodes intimacy as much as distrust or fear. It is the same with intimacy with God. The devil knows this. His name is the second word that helps us to benefit from James' instruction. Recall from Chapter 3 that *devil* in Greek means "slanderer." As a believer, you cannot be separated from God physically. So the enemy attempts to undermine intimacy by telling lies about God's character and yours. Usually, his scheme involves how you disappointed God by failing to satisfy some law. The so-called failure might be as simple as not checking something off a to-do list. It could be as religious as believing that what you ate disrespected your body as

God's temple. Sin is not necessarily involved. Any "have tos" are laws. When "have tos" become "I didn'ts," people tend to fear that God is disappointed or angry. This is what negatively affects any sense of closeness, and it is what the enemy stands by to instigate.

To grow and maintain intimacy with God, believers should follow James' advice to resist the devil as much as unbelievers. But how do you do that? Not by striving to do better. Not with more discipline. And not by remaining sin conscious. It is far more effortless than those religious hamster wheels. You repel the slanderer by remembering who God is and who you are to Him. Call to mind that God is love, and He loves you unfailingly and perfectly. In the words of the apostle John, "perfect love expels all fear" (1 John 4:18). This does not so much mean fear of spiders, heights, or public speaking. (Though knowing that you can trust God should help with those fears as well.) Ultimately, the truth of God's perfect, unfailing love for you banishes the fear that you are bad and God is mad (verse 18). It evicts the slanderer and grounds your relationship with God. No more spiritual rollercoaster rides! Furthermore, it removes the mental and emotional barriers to hearing God's voice and sensing His presence, even regarding things as eternally insignificant as a phone.

Remembering God's love for you is the key to feeling as close to Him as He really is. Nothing you do will change His love for you. Nothing you do will increase or decrease His presence with you. He does, however, desire that you live with Him in a particular way. You might be as stunned about this as Jesus' disciples were. Join me in the next chapter to discover what God wants most.

QUESTIONS FOR PERSONAL REFLECTION

1. How often do you hear God or sense His presence? When you do, how does He speak to you or guide you most commonly?

2. Do you experience a "rollercoaster relationship" with God? What patterns do you notice when God feels close or distant to you?

3. Think about the teachings and Scripture verses that have influenced how you relate with God. Are they intended for those under the old covenant of law or the new covenant of grace?

4. In what ways does your intimacy with God suffer from thoughts, fears, or feelings?

5. If you begin to feel distant from God, what are some truths you will remember about God and yourself?

7

What God Wants Most

Now you are no longer a slave but God's own child. —Galatians 4:7

If anyone should not have been hungry and homeless, it was this guy. He was the son of an exceptionally wealthy man. Nevertheless, he suddenly found himself having to convince a local farmer to hire him so that he could survive. He did not land the job because he stood at a street corner with a sign that read, "Will work for food." No, he was in too desperate of a condition to wait for some good-hearted person to pass by and offer help. He had to be proactive and persuasive, which was not difficult for him. As the youngest child, he grew up believing that he had to justify his place in his Jewish family. Convincing the farmer, therefore, was just another exercise in the same process.

I am not privy to everything about the young man's upbringing, except that I know his father had not instilled any sense that he had to prove himself. That notion came from their religious tradition—and typical sibling rivalry. At that time, first-born males received all the favor and honor. After all, they were the long-dreamed-of "anointed one" who made someone a father or a mother. Sometimes they were the first to make someone a grandparent. As the youngest of four boys, I can attest that these unconscious biases are not missed by the other siblings, even in modern families that are not Jewish; however, back then, they put their money where their mouths were. According to the Law, the oldest son in a family received a double share of their father's inheritance (see Deuteronomy 21:17). Every other son received only a single share.

Still, we are not talking about chump change here. With a dad like his, even a single share was significant. Everything in it could be sold for a fortune. He recognized that the money could buy his ticket out from the shadow of his older brother and the rules of their religion. He is hardly the only son in history to want that. With the charm and persuasive skills only a baby of the family could possess, he swayed his father to divide up the inheritance immediately. And far, far away he ran.

You will not be surprised to hear that he quickly ran himself right into the ground. Within no time, he had spent his newfound fortune on only God knows what. Within no time, he was pouring slop into a trough for hogs. Within no time, he was wishing he had never left home. Remembering that even his dad's employees had a better life than he presently did, he wondered if there was a way home. He figured that getting back in the family was a lost cause. With everything he had done, he felt unworthy to be called a son. But maybe he could return as a worker. Maybe he could re-earn his father's favor, or at the very least, make a little means to improve his situation. He had to take the chance.

Perhaps you have figured it out by now. If this story sounds familiar, it is because I just retold the first half of one of Jesus' most popular stories, but with some additional commentary of my own. It is most known as the parable of the Prodigal Son (see Luke 15:11–32). I once heard someone joke that it is the parable of the absent mother. (Where is she, anyway?) Jesus, however, used the story to emphasize someone else.

We know that Jesus did things to shock His original audience. Telling this story is one of those things. First, people would have been stunned to hear about a father who parted with all his possessions before his death while he still needed them. That stuns modern readers, too. These days, I know that some parents begin to share portions of their inheritance years before their death. Besides some tax benefits, they do this to see their children enjoy it. But I do not know of anyone who gives away everything while they are still alive. This dad did, though. Furthermore, he probably knew that doing so would fund his son's total misuse of freedom. Double shocking.

At least as perplexing is that when the son returned to the father, the father took him back easily. And not as a hired hand. Not even on probationary terms to prove his trust or repay what he had squandered. The father threw him a party to affirm and celebrate his place in the family, as if nothing had ever happened. Naturally, not everyone appreciated the fanfare. Especially not his older brother. He protested the unfairness of it all. "All these years I've slaved for you and never once refused to do a single thing you told me to. And in all that time you never gave me even one young goat for a feast with my friends" (verse 29).

Undoubtedly, Jesus intended His Jewish audience to see themselves in the older brother. He wanted them to recognize that, just like him, they, too, had mistakenly based their position with God on what they did for Him. Jesus also wanted some others to see themselves as the wandering and wayward younger brother. Both characters are as relatable to people today as they were when He first told the story. But Jesus especially desired for people to see God in the father. That is because seeing God as a father was a revolutionary idea back then.

Revealing the Father

Jesus did plenty to provoke the fury of religious leaders when He healed on the Sabbath. But when He challenged their rule by saying, "My Father is always working, and so am I" (John 5:17), they doubled down on their commitment to kill Him. The point of their contention was "My Father." They considered claiming equality with God to be blasphemous. They also believed that personalizing Him in such a way minimized His holiness.

I know that it is hard to understand the issue these days. You probably begin your prayers by addressing God as "Father." Most Christians do. But in the four thousand years before Jesus, God's people never addressed Him that personally.[1] Sure, there are occasions in the Old Testament in which a prophet referred to God as "our Father" or "Israel's

Father" (see Isaiah 63:16; Jeremiah 31:9). But those are formal descriptions that speak of God as the nation's founder or creator. In our culture, such a title might be compared to how Americans describe George Washington, Benjamin Franklin, John Adams, or Thomas Jefferson. We refer to each of them as a "founding father" because they helped to establish America as a country. But you would never think of one of them as your personal father. Not as someone who takes interest in your life or that you could speak to directly.

Can you imagine if you heard someone today refer to "my father, George Washington"? You might consider them disrespectful. You would surely think they are nuts. Yet this is precisely how Jesus spoke of God. Not just here or there, either. "Father" is how Jesus referred to God most frequently. To the religious leaders of His time, this was more than crazy—it was criminal. And it was further proof that He had a radical agenda that they needed to extinguish.

John's gospel exposes this agenda more than any other. Before I lead you to it, please keep in mind when I said in chapter 3 that each of the four gospels emphasize unique aspects of Jesus' ministry. This is the natural outcome of four different authors. God handpicked them so that the gospels together provide a complete picture of Jesus and what He achieved.

Matthew stresses how Jesus fulfilled Old Testament prophecy as the promised Messiah. That is why he began with such a detailed genealogy of Jesus. Mark offers a fast-paced account of Jesus' ministry. He skipped the details to get right to the main events. Luke provides eyewitness testimonies to prove Jesus' divinity and care for people. Compared to the others, however, John's gospel breaks the mold. It is considered the most theologically developed of all the gospels.

Maybe that is because it was written by Jesus' "beloved disciple," the one who knew His heart the most. In any case, from the first verse, the difference is noticeable. It does not begin with genealogy or a narrative of Jesus' birth. The gospel of John begins with a description of the inseparable relationship between Jesus and God. "In the beginning the Word already existed. The Word was with God, and the Word was God" (John 1:1). Throughout his gospel, he continues to build on this theme of relationship until it reaches a crescendo of extraordinary significance to all of us.

As a first point, God is referred to as "Father" most frequently in John's gospel. That is evident in just the first several chapters. To the merchants who sold sacrifices, Jesus attributes the temple as "my Father's house" (John 2:16). Prophesying about Jesus, John the Baptist remarks that "the Father loves his Son" (John 3:35). During the encounter with the Samaritan woman, Jesus discusses worshiping "the Father" (John 4:21). More instances exist than I can mention here. More than one hundred, in fact. These first three occasions, though, reflect how Jesus describes God until His resurrection. That is, Jesus revealed Him as "the Father" and "My Father." This is huge, of course. But in John's gospel, this is only the first half of His agenda. When Jesus rises from the dead, everything gets much more personal.

Imagine the scene on resurrection day. Before daybreak that Sunday morning, Mary Magdalene decides to pay a visit to Jesus' tomb. She notices something strange immediately. The stone to the entrance of the tomb is rolled away. The tomb is eerily vacant. Frustrated and confused, she hurries to alert the disciples. Frantic disbelief overtakes everyone. But they see for themselves that Mary is right. All that remains of Jesus are the wrappings and cloth that covered His bloody body. Like most humans, they go straight to the worst-case scenario. They are convinced that someone stole His body as another act of cruelty. Having no recourse and nowhere to turn, they leave devastated. They believe for a moment that Jesus is not only dead, but there is no body for them to mourn. But just for a moment.

Mary stays back to grieve. She finally manages to shed some tears when something interrupts her yet again. I cannot say if it is a divine unction, a woman's intuition, or what, but something tells her to double check the tomb. As she ducks her head in, she finds two white-robed men at each end. She does not seem to realize that they are angels. She questions them until another person outside the tomb catches her attention, whom she mistakes for a gardener. She turns to Him to express her concerns.

"Mary!" He says to calm her anxiety. It works. Something about the familiar way He says her name miraculously opens her eyes, unveiling who He is. It is Jesus! Talk about feeling all the feels. Mary went from grief, to confusion, to anger, back to grief, now to joy. Overcome by emotion, she throws herself at Him. Who can blame her? If I encountered a loved one back from the dead, I would do the same.

But Jesus does not allow her to cling to Him for long. He has a mission for Mary. "Go find my brothers," Jesus instructs her. "And tell them, 'I am ascending to my Father and your Father, to my God and your God'" (John 20:17). This is a revolutionary message. And Mary runs away quickly to spread it.

Do you wonder what is so significant or different about this moment and what Jesus said? For starters, He tasked a woman to give testimony to men. As if He hadn't smashed enough rules already, this was a whopper of one to shatter in those days. There is a message in it even for some people today. That message is bolstered by the fact that Jesus gave a woman the most world-changing message of all.

You see, His instruction to Mary marks the first time in John's gospel that Jesus described God as more than "my Father" or "the Father," but as *your* Father." In this, John's gospel reaches its crescendo! It is what he prepared his readers to see as the culmination of Jesus' incarnation. It is this: "All who believed him and accepted him, he gave the right to become children of God" (John 1:12). Revealing God as Father was enormous enough. It was yet another level to reveal that people could be His children.

How God's Children are Made

In biblical times, everyone understood that they came from something more than nature. There were no big bang or evolutionary theories. The apostle Paul maintained what all people believed in some way: the existence of creation itself is evidence of a creator (see Romans 1:20). Although the sun, moon, stars, trees, and everything else do not say who the Creator is or provide what is necessary for salvation, they are a step toward it. When people are reminded that they are their Creator's handiwork, they tend to want to know more about Him. This is how the apostle Paul caught the attention of unbelievers at Athens. "We are his offspring," Paul boasted. "In him we live and move and exist" (Acts 17:28).

Jewish people, of course, knew their Creator's name. Like I said earlier, they knew God as the nation's Father. They also knew that each person reflects Him in a special way. That truth was foundational from the beginning. The first chapter of the Bible affirms that "God created human beings in his own image" (Genesis 1:27). They understood that sin did not change this fact, either. That is because God reiterated the truth about His image in people some 1,600 years after sin infected creation (see Genesis 9:6). My point is, everyone knew that they came from a creator. What was revolutionary is that someone could become His child.

That might sound strange to most of us today. But as the New Testament writers meant it, being someone's "child" was not the same as being someone's offspring. They described the Roman process through which a wealthy father selected someone to whom he would pass on his family's inheritance. In other words, the father gave the "rights" to the family through something called "sonship" or "adoption" (see Romans 8:15; Ephesians 1:5).

At this point, I must caution you not to confuse this with our modern sense of adoption. In those days, adoption had nothing to do with a child being physically given to a new parent. It was about someone being chosen for a special union that offered irrevocable benefits. Through it, he literally received a new identity. Any of his previous debts or current or future obligations were canceled. There was nothing to prove or earn anymore. The blessings of the adopted father were available immediately and forever.[2]

Do you recognize the similarities from the prodigal son's story from earlier in this chapter? Just like the son, no one is truly fatherless. Both unbelievers and believers have a heavenly Father who created and loves them. Certainly, people rebel against Him and wander away from Him. This is often due to wrong beliefs that come from religion, but never from Him.

Helping people realize that God is good is therefore the first step to bringing them home. And when someone returns home by accepting God's goodness demonstrated by Jesus, they are celebrated instantly with "sonship." That is, they are united in personal relationship with God forever, forgiven of all debts, immediately relieved of any obligations, and instantly offered all His promises with no conditions. This is what it means to be a son or daughter of God, which changes everything about what God wants from you. He wants you to act like a child.

Acting Like a Child

Growing up, I watched many children grow up. My mom provided childcare for up to a dozen babies and toddlers every day at our house. I loved to hear the babbling of babies who discovered that they could make noises with their mouth. Other baby noises were not so enjoyable. Especially not as an adolescent on a summer morning when I wanted to sleep in. Those moments aside, my mom's daycare provided me with many fond memories that I will never forget. Some of my favorites were getting to hear a child's first word. Parents often bet on whose name their child would stutter first. The most frequent winner in my experience? Hands down, it was "dada." Obviously, the fathers took great pride in this. Though "mama" usually followed shortly thereafter.

I am sure that whatever parent's name a child says first has nothing to do with his or her favorite. It is likely what is easiest. I also know that what a child calls his or her mother or father is learned behavior. Babies do not know to say "mama" or "dada" instinctively. They are taught this. But it sticks. Most address their parents as "mom" or "dad" (or something similar) for the rest of their life. It is intimate. To call them anything else would seem impersonal and cold, even disrespectful. This is not only true for English-speaking countries, but it is true in every other culture. For example, German children often refer to a mom as *mutti* and a dad as *vati*. Brazilians use *mãe* and *pai*. Children in Israel call them *ima* and *abba*.[3]

Do you recognize that last one, *abba*? This is the name that Jesus used when He spoke to God directly. Just hours before He was arrested in the Garden of Gethsemane, with His fate on the cross heavy on His mind, He cried, "Abba, Father" (Mark 14:36). Interestingly, Mark chose to keep *abba* in Aramaic rather than translate it into Greek. He did this to emphasize the intimate nature of Jesus' relationship with God.[4] It is a glimpse into a raw, tender moment of a child confiding in His dad. This would not have gone unnoticed to people back then. It should not go unnoticed to us today.

Beyond how Jesus addressed God in prayer, He demonstrated a childlike relationship between Himself and the Father throughout the gospels. He encouraged people to approach God in the same way. On several occasions, in fact, He told His disciples that childlikeness is what God desires most. "Unless you turn and become like children, you will never enter the kingdom of heaven" (Matthew 18:3 ESV; see also Mark 10:15). In hearing this, be careful not to confuse "childlike" with "childish." To be childish is to be senseless and silly. Maybe even reckless and rebellious. Though God has grace for our growth, immaturity like that is not what Jesus meant. The childlike relationship with God that He modeled for us is one of trust and security rooted in intimacy with a good father—a good *dad*.

Sadly, I know that not everyone has experienced what it is like to have a good parent. But try to think of it this way. A child runs to hug her parent, sweaty from an afternoon of play with stains on her clothes and smelling like the outside. The child gives no thought to how she looks or smells. She does not fear that her parent will reject her. The child approaches her parent with not much more than the simple faith that she is welcomed and loved as she is. As the beloved children of a loving Father, God wants us to approach Him similarly.

Despite Jesus' encouragement, I find that "childlike" is the opposite of how many children of God go to Him today. Most approach God as only His servant. That was me. For years, I measured my maturity in the faith by what I did, gave, and sacrificed for Him. I also believed these things gauged how pleased God was with me and whether or not He would bless me.

But that is not how you relate to a good father. That is how you relate to a slave master. If Jesus' actions and words do not convince you that God wants a different kind of relationship with you, then Paul's words should clarify it. "Now you are no longer a slave but God's own child" (Galatians 4:7).

This is not about being idle or inactive. Christians do lots of things. We give of our time, talents, and treasures in service to God and to help advance His message. Paul did. In response to God's goodness and love, it was his pleasure to serve God. He did not, however, serve God to earn His pleasure or goodness. He served with the delight of one who already has God's pleasure and goodness. That is the right, childlike approach we all should have in whatever we do for God.

Here is the bottom line that Jesus came to reveal: what matters most to God is not what you do for Him, but who you are to Him. God is your good Father, and you are His beloved child. Amazingly, this means that like Jesus you, too, get to call God, "Abba, Father" (Romans 8:15), and enjoy all the acceptance and approval that comes with it. If you do nothing else, that is enough. But you might be surprised what becoming God's child did inside of you, which empowers you to do so much more. Things are about to get very personal.

QUESTIONS FOR PERSONAL REFLECTION

1. Do you relate more to the older brother or to the prodigal son in the parable of the good father? Why?
2. What metrics have you used to assess your relationship with God up to this point? How has doing so affected your relationship with Him?
3. Describe your relationship with your earthly father. How is it different from or similar to Jesus' description and demonstration of God as Father?
4. What does it mean to you to know that you are adopted by God? What debts or obligations should you see yourself freed from? What benefits should you begin to enjoy?
5. How would it look to be more childlike in your relationship with God?

Enough Is Enough

So you also are complete through your union with Christ. —Colossians 2:10

"Kyle, I need help!"

This appeared at the top of my phone around six o'clock one Tuesday morning. It was a message from someone who knows me well enough to know that I would be wide awake by then. But also, someone who knows to try me with a text before a phone call. Now that is a good friend!

"What's up?" I replied within seconds of the new-message ding. I watched as the typing indicator inside the app appeared then disappeared a few times within a couple of minutes. It seemed to me that he was figuring out how to say something. Then it came through.

"I went to update my LinkedIn profile last night, but I just stared at my computer for hours." I was a bit relieved. This was not exactly the emergency that I feared it might be just a few minutes earlier. Still, I thought it warranted a phone call in return.

My friend answered with a tone in his voice that somehow signaled to me that he had been up for more than a few hours. Sure enough, I was right. He went on to confess that he had struggled all night to present himself in a way that would attract future opportunities.

As an author, I have learned a thing or two about writer's block. To help my friend get his thoughts to flow, I began to ask him about some of his accomplishments.

"You earned a doctorate, right?"

"Two, actually," he replied.

"And in what locations have you lived since you graduated?"

"Washington, D.C., Seattle, and London," he answered in the same matter-of-fact manner as he had responded to my previous question. I reminded him that he also had been honored recently as a top performer at his job.

"You have plenty to tout on a résumé," I assured.

"I know," he acknowledged. "I have all of that listed already."

"What's the issue, then?" I questioned.

"It all feels not enough. *I* feel not enough," he clarified through cracks in his voice. "What do I do?"

Unfortunately, feeling not enough, lacking, unworthy, unqualified—whatever you want to call it—is something about which I also know a great deal. I am here to walk you through what I have learned that helped me answer my friend's question.

But first, when you hear his concern, do you think, "What does he have to feel lacking about?" After all, before he was forty, he had lived across the world, achieved the highest level of education in two fields, and was awarded for his performance in his career. Most people see someone like him as the definition of enough. Most people also think of movie and music stars, multi-millionaire business moguls, and bestselling authors as the quintessential definition of enough. Yet despite their accomplishments, accolades, awards, and affluence, these people struggle with this insecurity as much as anyone else. Oftentimes more so.

I think of something I heard once from Tom Hanks. Surely you know his name from one of the more than seventy films and movies he has acted in so far. It is rumored that his award-winning career has amassed him a fortune of more than $400 million. Most people would consider even a half percent of that as enough. Hanks admitted, however, that he still doubts himself constantly. He confessed, "No matter what we've done, there comes a point where you think, 'How did I get here? When are they going to discover that I am, in fact, a fraud?'"[1]

The stories I shared represent one of the most human things. Everyone seeks legitimacy. We yearn to feel worthy, to overcome an innate sense of wrongness, and to be enough. Don't you? These are not evil wants. God wants these for you, too. But because of our shame nature, we try to attain these in ways that God never designed. Achieving fame and fortune is one way people attempt fulfillment. Others believe that earning a title, an education, being married, having children, or owning a house will make them someone. Some measure their meaning by their involvement and service. Church folk are especially susceptible to that. Yet a lesson we can learn from many celebrities and high achievers is that no amount of performance and what it achieves can quench the want for worth, rightness, and significance. They were not designed to.

I do not, of course, mean to discourage you from pursuing these good things. If you desire education, marriage, children, or a home, then by all means go after them. Be involved in your church and community, too. But see these feats for what they are, which are fruit *from* you, not the root *of* you. That is, they do not make you. They do not measure anything about you. They do not make God any more pleased with you than He already is, either. Many throughout history have learned this lesson the hard way, myself included. I stressed out and nearly burned out trying to prove what Jesus had already proved.

The Proof of Your Worth

I stood nervously at the back of the church while a couple of hundred people sat and gawked at me. Even though this would not be all that unusual in a charismatic church, it was a new experience for me. I was seventeen years old, and a guest preacher had asked me to stand because he claimed to have a word for me from God. Keep in mind that I was barely a year into my born-again faith. This was my first encounter with something like this. I did not know what to expect. My knees shook in fear that my every sin might be exposed in front of everyone. Nothing felt scarier than that at the time, trust me.

Thankfully, the man did not humiliate me as I feared. Nobody who really hears from God would do something like that, because God does not do something like that. He, instead, affirmed something in me. It was a call to ministry that, just months before, I had also begun to sense. After he rattled off a handful of Scripture verses that collectively described God's plan for me, the preacher concluded, "You are the church *yacker*."

His prophetic word made sense of my newfound passion for the faith, but *yacker* was far from reality. In my elementary years, I was afraid to talk to people. Most days I played alone at recess. Even through junior high, I frequently sat alone at the lunch table and was chosen last for groups and teams. Shy? Outcast? Insecure? Absolutely. But *yacker*? Absolutely not. Nobody would have said that about me. But this man did. He claimed that God had. I decided to believe it. But for it to become true, I believed that I had a lot to prove and perfect. This was all part of the next decade of my life, which culminated in the "What more do I have to do?" question with which I opened this book.

At the time, nobody told me explicitly that I had to prove myself to God. Certainly not my pastor or youth pastors. I got this from a mixture of influences. Culture itself was partly culpable. Do-to-get is the philosophy upon which the world spins. And I do mean spins. My childhood religious tradition undoubtedly played a part, too. It was ingrained into me from birth that God is pleased when we meet obligations and discipline ourselves. That kind of programming can take many years, if not a lifetime, to unravel completely. Add to all that a deeply seated rejection complex that convinced me that acceptance comes from accomplishment. I was already inclined to performance-based living before reading any books or hearing any sermons.

But then I did read books, and I heard many more sermons. I acknowledge that I probably misunderstood some of them. Though not all. Many blatantly communicated a message that only reinforced this inclination to qualify myself.

Especially if I was to be used by God as a mouthpiece, a *yacker*. I have already shared the ups and downs that this produced in me. Some days I felt good. Most days I felt like a total fraud. I did not know it back then, but that is the end result of anything that is performance based. There is no other possible outcome. Remember, flesh is destined to fail. And relying on it is designed to bring you to your breaking point.

Naturally, how long it takes for someone to arrive at this point varies vastly from person to person. I know people who reached their breaking point after only a year or two of striving. Others took thirty years or more. The timing comes down to how long it takes for people to feel that they have exhausted all their options and realize that those options have not worked. For me, it took about a decade after my born-again experience. At first, when every super-spiritual method in the book did not produce what I expected, I thought something was permanently wrong with me. I feared I was unworthy of being a child of God, much less of my calling. I almost gave up on it. Almost.

During one of the lowest dips in my faith journey—a time when I felt exceptionally worthless and was days away from quitting—I happened to read a book that highlighted John the Baptist's proclamation at Jesus' baptism. You know, the one we explored a few chapters ago: "Behold, the Lamb of God, who takes away the sin of the world" (John 1:29 ESV). This was not a new verse to me. By this time in my life, I was almost finished with seminary. But the circumstances of the moment made me see it as I never had. It brought me face-to-face with the cross. What happened is another story entirely, but suffice it to say that, in a matter of minutes, I beheld that there was so much more to what Jesus did than I ever knew.[2]

You see, for as long as I can remember, I understood that Jesus died to forgive my sins. At sixteen years old, I was reacquainted with this truth in a deeply personal way. Still, almost all I really knew about the cross was what it meant about my past. I never considered its implications for my present or future, aside from getting me into heaven. But this encounter set me on a course to see that Jesus accomplished everything for which the human soul seeks.

First and foremost, I was struck by the extent to which Jesus went for humanity. I always knew He suffered. A statue of Him on the cross hung at the front of my childhood church. But in this encounter, when I beheld the brutality of it, I beheld the unconditional love of it. It made something He did from the cross so poignant to me. Through streams of blood that ran down over His eyes like tears, He looked over the people who put Him there with mercy. Then He pleaded, "Father, forgive them, for they don't know what they are doing" (Luke 23:34).

Do you see the magnitude of grace in this single act? In response to the mocking and the torture He received from these people, He forgave them. Receiving no apologies, He forgave them. Getting no promises of change, He forgave them. But not just them. He put Himself through the mutilation of the cross for everyone—past, present, and future—with no conditions or expectations. "While we were still sinners" is how the apostle Paul put it. Why would Jesus do that? Paul revealed it was to prove God's love for us (see Romans 5:8). All of us.

To put it personally, Jesus went to the greatest extreme to show that you are worth something. Just as you are. Before any accomplishments, accolades, or effort on your part. Just by virtue of your existence as someone made in God's image. The cross is the ultimate proof of your worth.

The mere thought of that revelation brought me to tears after my encounter, first on my living room floor and then at times while driving. For weeks later, I remember driving with sunglasses on cloudy days just so passersby did not see my spontaneous sobs. It was that huge for me—and that healing. But it was only the kick start to accepting what Paul added is an even greater benefit: the cross makes people permanently right and pleasing to God (see Romans 8:9–11).

The Whole and Holy You

This might sound like a strange analogy at first. When it came to Jesus and me, I always thought of myself as a countertop and Him as a cleaning spray, such as Lysol. I knew that because of the cross, He was able to cleanse sin. And I believed that He did cleanse me upon my salvation. But if your countertops are anything like mine, they do not stay clean for long. For one, environmental debris like dust begins to collect instantly without my consent. But also, I inevitably splatter pancake batter, orange juice, and bacon grease when making breakfast. Dinnertime is worse. Even if I were to attach a can of Lysol to my hip and spritz and scrub after every mess, it would be impossible to keep them clean entirely.

Spritzing and scrubbing after every mess is essentially how I used Jesus. It was very transactional. When I failed, I begged, "Please cleanse me again, Lord!" I always believed that He did, but it did not take long for me to feel dirty again.

If not because of myself, then because of my environment. So, rinse and repeat. That regimen got exhausting. Mostly because it never satisfied that innate feeling of wrongness in me. In fact, sometimes it increased the feeling that I was a complete and utter fraud. Yet it is all that I knew to do.

Here is a quick review from the first half of this book: humans are incapable of perfection, and God knows it. First, we are each born with an inherited predisposition to sin—a sin nature that was passed down to us from Adam. Secondly, flesh fails, and it always will. Thirdly, we live in a fallen world. Simply put, we are darned if we do and darned if we don't. This is why God sent Jesus to do more than cleanse sin every time we ask. Or as some put it, to enable us to "keep a short sin account." Recall that the apostle Paul revealed that because of the cross, God no longer counts our sins against us (see 2 Corinthians 5:19). This means that your failures do not collect in some account (or on some countertop) until God wipes them away again. You stay clean.

This is about far more than being let off the hook for our humanity, though. It is that because of the cross, Jesus provided a way to change our humanity. Paul described what happens upon belief as a kind of spiritual identity change. He boasted, "Anyone who belongs to Christ has become a new person" (2 Corinthians 5:17). Still a person, of course. And still capable of failure. Just not defined by it. As a believer, you are defined, instead, as someone who is right (see verse 21). Again, not until your next mistake, but forever. More about all of that later. For now, understand that this means that despite wrong feelings, you are a right person. It means that despite wrong memories, you are a right person. It means that despite wrong symptoms, you are a right person. It means that despite a wrong history, you are a right person. I like to say it this way: Christ rights you despite you.[3]

You are not alone if you are perplexed by this. It has baffled even the best minds since Jesus ascended into heaven. Not because people think it is impossible for God to change someone. After all, God spoke the entire universe into existence. So surely, He can remake someone in an instant, too. The issue for many people is that being made completely right by faith alone seems too easy on our part. Yet Paul insisted that this effortless change is exactly what Jesus came to provide.

Paul devoted much of his ministry to defending and explaining the wonder of it. He especially spelled it out to the Christians at Colossae who were being challenged by religious leaders that they needed much more than faith in Jesus to please God.[4] They argued for a return to certain traditions. Paul rejected their "empty philosophies and high-sounding nonsense" (his words, not mine), maintaining that Jesus provided people with all they need because of the cross. "For in Christ lives all the fullness of God in a human body. So you also are complete through your union with Christ" (Colossians 2:8–10).

In this single revelation, Paul encapsulated everything that it means to be a believer—a child of God. It is completion. I am not sure that words can describe this adequately. In fact, I know that they cannot. What I can say, though, is that Jesus is everything that God wanted. Everything that God required. Everything that is right and pleasing to God. He is also all peace, all patience, all joy, and all love—all good.

When you said yes to Jesus, everything that was wrong about you was replaced with everything about Him (see verses 10–11). Through this union with Him, you were instantly made new, made right, made whole, and made holy. As far as God is concerned, you lack nothing. There is nothing left for you to earn. There is nothing left for you to prove. This means something that was especially freeing for me: there is nothing that you need to fix.

No Need for Fixing

In chapter 3, I said that God enjoys leading us on a process of discovery. This not only includes leading us to see who He is, but also to see who we are in Him. He often begins with worth, then righteousness, then completion in Christ. I suppose that each revelation is necessary for the next. And God is so good that He knows just the right timing for us to receive these truths. That is how it has been for me, at least. My encounter at the cross was profound, and it was what ultimately opened my eyes to His love and grace. From that awakening, I continued to discover so much more over a period of years. My growth is evident in the messages I have taught and the books I have written. I expect to grow in my understanding of His love and grace forever.

Though I recognized quickly how far God went to prove His love, and I found my worth in the fact that I was made in His image, my understanding of being right and complete in Him took longer to develop. I still believed there was much about me that God needed me to fix. Especially if I was to grow into this long-term promise for which I had been believing since high school.

One of them was my personality. I did not think an introvert could be a *yacker*. Many of the other *yackers* who ministered in the churches I attended over the years came with stories of how they nearly led the entire airplane to the Lord on the way to the church. Yet to this day, when a stranger attempts to speak to me on a flight, I think, *Would you please shut up?*

Do not get me wrong. I care about people and love to speak to people in groups. The larger the crowd the better, in fact. But I do not enjoy one-on-one interaction with people I hardly know. This means that I am not so quick to pray for people on the spot. And I do not enjoy street evangelism. For years, I considered myself flawed for this. I sometimes wondered, *Can I even be a Christian and not like to do these things?* I tried to change, but I never got very far.

To be clear, I no longer believe that being an introvert is something to be fixed. I think it is one of many God-given traits with which He graces people for a purpose. That is a topic for the next chapter. On the way to me getting here, however, God used this "struggle" to reveal to me what it means to be complete in Christ and yet have a weakness in some area. Who cannot relate to having a real or perceived weakness? We all can. Even our favorite Bible heroes can, like the apostle Paul.

While Paul developed his theology of what it means to be complete in Christ, he came to terms with some things about himself that did not change. He admitted to moments of weakness. He spoke of an obstacle that did not go away regardless of how much he prayed (see 2 Corinthians 12:8). We do not know to what extent Paul grappled with this. We do know, however, that he did not try to forever fix himself. He concluded that the same grace that saved him is enough to keep him and empower him. When it came to remaining lovable, qualified for God's promises, and able to fulfill God's plans, he recognized that God's grace is enough (see verse 9).

I learned from Paul's story that our union with Christ means that He makes up for every area of our flesh that falls short. He fills in our gaps and cracks with His grace. I think of this like *Kintsugi* pottery. *Kintsugi* is a Japanese word that means "golden repair." I am sure you have seen some of this kind of pottery in photos. A classic example is a broken bowl with its pieces mended together by gold. The Japanese like to showcase this art as a reflection of their philosophy that strength, beauty, and wholeness come from embracing flaws and imperfections.[5]

Whether they know it or not, the Japanese have tapped into a profound biblical truth. We are each clay jars that are born uniquely broken (see 2 Corinthians 4:7). And the vices of life crack us even further. But we are beautifully restored to wholeness by the redemptive power of the One who loves us through it all (see Hebrews 10:14). This, of course, does not mean that your issues are all resolved in a literal sense or that you would not benefit from addressing some of those issues in practical ways such as through diet, counseling, or medicine. It would benefit my health, for example, to fix my aversion to vegetables. The thing is that to God, you are not a person in *need* of fixing. You are someone already made whole by the gold of His grace.

Friend, Jesus accomplished everything that means anything about you. He proved your worth. He made you right. He qualified you for all of God's promises. In Him, you are enough. More than enough, really. As a result of grabbing hold of this truth, I have experienced healing in ways I never imagined possible. It freed me to maximize my uniqueness without shame and to experience purpose without stress or striving. I know that it will do the same for you, too.

That brings me to how I answered my friend's question when he asked, "What do I do?" I told him, "Just be you. That is what got you this far. It is the key to your future success, too." Let's talk about that in the next chapter.

QUESTIONS FOR PERSONAL REFLECTION

1. In what areas of your life have you felt as though you were a fraud, an impostor, unworthy, or unqualified?

2. What material things, worldly means, or spiritual solutions have you used to try to define or measure yourself? What was the result?

3. As a reflection of God's image, every human has worth and value. Do you find this easy or difficult to accept for yourself? Why?

4. Previously, in what circumstances did you believe you were "right"? When you felt that you lost this status, how did you attempt to regain it?

5. How have you tried to please God by fixing your weaknesses or imperfections? What will you do differently after reading this chapter?

9

Designed to Be Different

For we are God's masterpiece. He has created us anew in Christ Jesus, so we can do the good things he planned for us long ago. —Ephesians 2:10

I grew nervous from the congregation's response when I asked, "Who feels as though they do not fit a mold?" Blank expressions. "Raise your hand if you feel as if you are a square peg trying to fit into a round hole," I clarified. The room remained still. For almost ten long seconds, I feared the point of my message was doomed from the beginning. Then one person raised their hand sheepishly, as if admitting a secret sin. Within seconds, a few more popped up with a bit less hesitancy. Soon, everyone in the church held their hands in the air, admitting proudly that they feel as though they do not fit in some way. I was relieved.

Though it was a slow start, the people proved my point far better than I imagined. I have learned over the years that everyone fears that their differences count them out of some group—sometimes every group. I thought people would be quick to admit that. Rookie mistake. I should have expected they would be afraid to admit it at first. That is because most of us feel ashamed of our differences. We worry that they make us someone who is wrong. As we explored in the last chapter, there is tremendous relief that comes from knowing what God did to make you right. There is freedom once you know that God does not expect you to fit a mold and when you embrace that He made you unique to do something unique.

"That's a modern message!" someone once complained to me. They asserted that the Bible does not say this. I acknowledge that this may not exactly be stated in a single Bible verse. Yet the truth that we are each handcrafted for a unique purpose is affirmed through the message of Scripture. Not to mention by the stories of the people in it. A psalm that King David wrote says as much. He praised that God "made all the delicate, inner parts of my body and knit me together in my mother's womb" (Psalm 139:13).

David's words, of course, do not only express a truth about himself. We all were knit together in our mother's womb. Besides, the phrase "knit together" does not illustrate some assembly-line process that produces duplicate after duplicate. No, David described an intricate and purposeful process through which God makes someone "wonderfully complex" (verse 14).

What Makes You, You

Not that we need it to, but modern science confirms our complexity more with every passing day. Those who study human identity have so far found dozens of different characteristics that make a person, each with characteristics inside of characteristics.[1] There are the obvious physical traits such as hair, eye and skin color, and height. These alone account for an endless amount of uniqueness. But there is a universe of immaterial differences within each of us. Personality, interests, talents, tastes, and intellectual abilities, just to name a few.

Some of your characteristics are so interconnected that they affect each other. Your cultural experiences and personality type, for example, influence how you think. How you think determines what you see. It is fascinating. Your brain interprets the data that your eyes send it.[2] This is why two people look at the same object or situation and see it completely differently. Some see the glass half full. Others see it half empty. Some see the solution to the problem as more government. Others see the solution as less government. And on and on. The conclusions people come to are just one outcome of our complex design.

Not everything about you is God's design. We live in a fallen world in which many things are not the way God originally intended. Disabilities and diseases are a case in point. God did not divvy these out to people for any reason. Some things about you are the product of genetic discrepancies that were passed down through your family. Others are the natural consequences of yours or someone else's actions. Debates over which qualities are the result of nature versus nurture are interesting, but they do not change anything. That is because God is not surprised by anything about you.

David also reflected on this truth. "You saw me before I was born," he said. "Every day of my life was recorded in your book. Every moment was laid out before a single day had passed" (Psalm 139:16). Here again, David is no different than anyone else. God encouraged the prophet Jeremiah similarly. "I knew you before I formed you in your mother's womb" (Jeremiah 1:5).

You should take those words to heart for yourself. You began as a plan in the mind of God. Then He formed you with qualities to fit that plan. Some were immediately evident at your birth. Others are discovered throughout your life. What is more, before a single cell of you existed, God saw how your life would play out, every single day of it. He knew about every failure, bad decision, and wrong turn.

That is not to say that He is happy that they happened (or will happen). But He is not upset with you about them, either. He prepared for them. Amazingly, God accounted for all the complexities and complications that make you, you. His plan for you included a way to redeem and repurpose those parts of you that He did not mean for you. God made a way to clean the dirty. To fix the broken. To take the ugly and make it beautiful. This is called the plan of salvation. Jesus was there, ready and waiting, to make all things new. Kind of.

Your Custom-Made Identity

"You promised that all things become new," I protested to God one day. "But why do I still wrestle with these old things?" I lodged this complaint when I was still in the fix-it mode of my faith. I could not understand why God did not change everything that I feared stood in the way of His plan for me.

Is there something about you that has not changed since you became a Christian? That is a ridiculous question. There are many things that did not change. Most obviously, your eye and skin color. The shape of your face. You probably did not lose your accent. I am willing to bet that your memories were not erased and that your personality type remained the same, too.

Please understand that I do not mean to imply that we should not expect transformation. Upon my coming to faith at sixteen years old, I received a new passion and desire for the things of God. I wanted to read His Word. I wanted to do right. I wanted to love people. I wanted to be used by God. And I did grow in boldness. Things really did change in me, and in huge ways. I know people who have experienced real, legit miracles and deliverances, too. God does all of that. But God will not change something about you that He designed in the first place.

I came to realize much of my stress (and what I often mistook for spiritual warfare) was from fighting God's design for me. You see, since childhood, I experienced that my differences caused rejection. This made me believe that qualities like my introverted personality were wrong. This was only reinforced by the rumpus revivals I attended later where boisterousness was admired as evidence of anointing. For years, I tried to fix what was never broken. This was frustrating because it was futile.

You might wrestle for the same reason. Trust me, you will forever struggle if you try to change God's designs. Or try to make right what is not wrong. Or try to perfect what is not imperfect. Besides, God's promise that "anyone who belongs to Christ has become a new person" (2 Corinthians 5:17) is not about a physical change anyway. It is about the spiritual transformation that made you a child of God. We have already discussed the instant forgiveness, acceptance, and approval that this gave you and how it completed you with the nature of Jesus. As if all of that is not huge enough, there is something more that happened that added to your uniqueness. You received spiritual gifts.

The apostle Paul explained that "in his grace, God has given us different gifts for doing certain things well" (Romans 12:6). Notice the words "different" and "certain." You are not expected to do all things well, nor to do certain things as well as someone else. They will not do certain things as well as you, either. We are each gifted differently by God for different reasons. Paul offered some examples: prophesy, service, teaching, encouragement, giving, leadership, and kindness (see verses 6–8).

Those are just a handful of the practical gifts. He described others that are more spiritual in nature, though equally as necessary. These include wisdom, words of knowledge, faith, healing, and working miracles (see 1 Corinthians 12:7–10). We also know from the Old Testament that God graces people with craftsmanship, artistic expression, and an eye for design (see Exodus 31:1–6). These are all categories. Nobody has a comprehensive list of every specific ability that God offers. He gifts people according to the needs in the world, which changes with each generation.

I know that there is an unspoken idea that every Christian should watch the same news channel, wear the same jeans (is skinny, holey, or oversized in style right now?), enjoy the same music, be passionate about the same causes, etc. Okay, maybe that is not so unspoken. In some circles, adherence to certain standards like these is a celebrated litmus test for Christianity. Cookie-cutter Christianity. That is as naïve as it is unbiblical. While we profess the same Jesus and possess the same Spirit, that is just about where our similarities end. You are not meant to fit a mold. Like every Christian, you are made to be a unique expression of the God who designed you. Stress and striving are the results of fighting your uniqueness. Effortless satisfaction and success are the results of embracing it.

The Secret to Effortless Success

A young guy in his mid-twenties asked to schedule a call with me. By this time, I had learned a preacher trick: never agree to a meeting before knowing the purpose for it. "Getting into ministry," he said, with a hopefulness in his voice that I admired. It reminded me of myself when I was his age. I am grateful for those who spoke into my life back then. I was happy to be that person for him.

We connected on a video call a week later. After the usual small talk and niceties (that I still hate but have grown better at), he asked his question. "How do I get started in ministry?" He shared about a budding social media platform and some online marketing courses he had completed. He was contemplating Bible school. Even through the low quality of a webcam and dim lighting, I could see the glimmer in his eyes from a bright future. He was looking for tangible steps, the secret sauce to ministry success.

I have a bit of a marketing background. I can talk branding, strategies, and systems all day long. There is nothing wrong with learning tactical ways to reach people. I decided to give him something very different, though.

"Maximize your differences," I offered. The furrow of his brow told me that I needed to elaborate. "Lean into the qualities about yourself that seem a bit weird, unconventional, even imperfect." That did not help. I think it scared him. To be fair, it would have scared me at his age, too. Usually, oddities and imperfections are the fodder of our insecurities. They are what we fear count us out. We try to hide them, not reveal them. Yet I have discovered those things that we are concerned will count us out are often what God uses to count us in—into His plan.

Anyone who understands marketing knows the power of the *gimmick*. I tend to cringe when I hear that word. It simply means something that attracts attention. But these days, it is often a trick that attracts attention. Consider some of the celebrities who wear outrageous clothing (or little-to-no clothing). They use their looks as a gimmick to stand out. Others take on flamboyant personas. Others use sensational headlines. People use these because they work. Heads turn, ears tune in, and fingers tap on things that stand out or appeal to human desires. Until the new wears off, at least. People who depend upon tricks must resort to more outrageous tricks to keep people's attention. That explains so much of what we see in the media today.

When it comes to fulfilling God's plan for your life, tricks are not necessary. God has equipped you with everything you need to do His will (see 2 Peter 1:3; Hebrews 13:21). Some of it was given to you at your conception. Some of it was added to you at your salvation. And even what was not given to you by God was repurposed at your salvation. As Paul boasted, "He has created us anew . . . so we can do the good things he planned for us long ago" (Ephesians 2:10). You do not need to strive to make that plan happen.

To help the promising young preacher understand my point, I shared with him about a series of insecurities that I faced at the beginning of ministry—all the ways I believed that I did not fit the mold of a contemporary preacher. My more introverted personality was only one aspect of it. At the time, hipster ministers were going viral. They spoke in "yo" and "bro" kind of language. I did not. I am more of an old soul than a millennial.

I also noticed that many came from a long line of ministers. Their daddy was a preacher. And so was their daddy's daddy. They had a foundation to build upon and the support to do so. Not so in my case. My calling broke the old family tradition. It took years to gain my family's support for what I do today. Furthermore, I did not have the same lifestyle as the others. It seemed to me that every successful preacher in their thirties or older had a wife, a kid, and a dog. Again, not me. I am not married. I do not have children. And just two months with a dog confirmed what I have always known: I am not an animal person.

Besides my stint with a dog, I revealed to him about some of the ways that I tried to change myself to fit the mold. "None of them worked," I admitted. "Some felt constricting, and others came across awkward." At the height of my frustration, I received some advice that set me free. I did not get it from a mentor. It came through a thought that I believe was from God. *Why don't you just be you?* I heard. *You have a unique personality, style, and story that can reach people others can't. Use the gift of you.*

Me—a gift? I had never thought such a thing. I certainly did not think my differences contributed to that. But I had no other choice than to embrace myself, which understanding my righteousness in Christ prepared me to do.

"Being *me* made all the difference," I told the guy. "Any influence that I have in ministry so far is a result of it." My conversation with him gave me the opportunity to reflect upon some of it. My insecurities led me to create ministry tools like the *Shut Up, Devil* app. The story of those insecurities also gave me a message and an audience.

It was once embarrassing for me to mention the rejection and mind games that I suffered in my youth. But as I began to hint about them—first on social media, then more openly through my teachings and books—more and more people tuned in. People said that they related to my experiences. In time, I also discovered that my innate interest in technology has its place in my plan, too. What made me a nerd in school fits me for ministry in this digital age. It is all so clear in hindsight. My greatest contributions to this world have come from leaning into the things that make me, me.

I encourage you in the same way that I encouraged the young man on the call. Do not despise your differences—maximize them. I know preachers who never liked the sound of their voice. Yet they found that their voice is what God uses to draw people's attention. The same may be true of any physical feature or personality trait that you have. God may use aspects of your story to do this, too. I do not mean that you should air everything about your life to the world. That is not always helpful. But coupled with your natural and spiritual gifts, even the qualities that you hate about yourself can make you a powerful gift. And they can lead you to what God always had in mind for you.

What Your Differences Do

Fulfilling purpose is a hot topic these days. You can find countless books, sermons, conferences, and courses that sell the steps to it. A "find your purpose" message is its own kind of gimmick, though. It appeals to the human tendency to equate accomplishment with significance. It also exploits our fear of missing out. Nothing but stress and striving come from that.

Do not get me wrong. I believe God has specific plans for specific people. Scripture is clear about that. It is also clear that God's plans are fulfilled naturally as someone remains true to themselves. Our God-given design and gifts orient us toward our purpose. Plus, He directs our steps (see Psalm 37:23). This means that purpose just . . . happens. The stories of a few prominent people in the New Testament demonstrate this in ways that should encourage you.

Your differences lead you to others like you.

Jesus' disciples were quite the motley crew. He purposefully chose misfits, outcasts, and people who would raise the eyebrows of the religious. Matthew was especially eyebrow raising. He was a Jewish tax collector. And those two identities—Jewish and tax collector—were not supposed to go together. To be one was to be a traitor, a cheater, a sinner of the highest order.

Matthew was not hiding his profession when Jesus recruited him. He was in the middle of it. But what the religious saw as a scandal, Jesus saw as an opportunity. "Follow me," Jesus shouted toward him while he sat in his tax collector's booth (Matthew 9:9). I can only imagine Matthew's thoughts. Perhaps it was something like, "Who me? I don't fit the mold to follow You." Yet he dared to accept Jesus' invitation.

I do not believe that God created Matthew as a cheat. In the same way, I do not believe that God creates anyone for any sinful profession. But Matthew is a great example of how God repurposes someone's past to relate His goodness to others who have a similar story. That is the first of many ways that God used him. Matthew immediately invited Jesus to a dinner party where "many tax collectors and other disreputable sinners" were introduced to Him (verse 10). Your story has the same power to introduce people to the love and goodness of God. That is Him working with human nature. We naturally attract and relate to others like us.

Your differences take you where God wants you.

The apostle Paul's past is well known. He persecuted Christians. Most famously, he oversaw the moment when Stephen was rocked to sleep—err, stoned to death (see Acts 7:59–60). Paul was driven by a penchant for truth, which he sometimes took to extremes. Zealous is how he described himself (see Galatians 1:14). After his dramatic conversion, his life changed profoundly. His thinking changed. His desires changed. His attitude changed. But his over-the-top personality did not. For good reason. God used it to fulfill His plan.

Considering Paul's history as a "pharisee of pharisees," you might assume that God called him to the Jews. Who better to enlighten Jewish people than someone so well versed in Judaism? Preaching to Jews is how he began. And God continued to use him to preach to them. His temperament, however, made him easily frustrated with their insistent opposition. After enduring a day of insults, he had had enough. "Your blood is upon your own heads," he exclaimed. "From now on I will go preach to the Gentiles" (Acts 18:6). And the rest is history. All his missionary journeys were to Gentile areas, where he planted at least fourteen churches. He wrote most of his letters to Gentiles. He was the apostle to the Gentiles. It is what he was born to do (see Galatians 1:15–16).

I know that there was much behind Paul's decision to go to the Gentiles. Undoubtedly, though, his personality initially helped to get him there. And when he got there, he realized how uniquely suited he was to reach them. As a Mosaic-Law scholar who was classically educated by Romans, he was gifted to teach Scripture in a way that Greeks could understand. His background also gave him Roman citizenship, which opened many doors in that world. Do you see? God used every aspect of Paul's life, even his rough edges, to accomplish what he was born to do.

He will do the same with you. Your personality, your pedigree, your style, your story—they all play a role in your plan. Together, they have a unique power to reflect God to people who need to see Him. That is surefire purpose. But I propose there might be another reason for your differences: to shock people.

Molded to Break a Mold

Religious people tend to believe that they have God figured out. Many are sure about who He will use and who He will not use. Who is in and who is out. It seems that God enjoys shattering their expectations. The company that Jesus kept is enough evidence of that. But God did not stop with His disciples. He continues to choose "things the world considers foolish" (1 Corinthians 1:27) to shock the wise. Paul's young missionary partner, Timothy, is my favorite example of this.

Do you know Timothy's story? He helped Paul reach the Gentiles in a significant way. Tradition says that he became the bishop of the church of Ephesus. Legalists would have never considered him qualified for any of this, though, because of the way that he was born. His mother was Jewish, and his father was Greek (see Acts 16:1). His Jewish contemporaries thought of him as a half-breed. Their rules barred him from many things, such as being educated with other Jewish boys and participating in Jewish festivals. He was different.

Human wisdom would have suggested a more mainstream candidate. A pure-blooded Jewish family man may have better fit the church-growth business plan. God, however, was not interested in quick growth by kowtowing to tradition. There was legalism to break! People were still arguing over food and circumcision laws. Some contended that Gentile converts needed to submit to Jewish law. God responded by raising up someone whose very existence broke their rules. He used Timothy to advance the Church!

Your differences could be part of God's plan to do the same today. Consider that you were molded to break a mold. Maybe, just maybe, your life is meant to express how God chooses and uses people that people never think He would. That is huge purpose! Whatever the case, this is certain: you were designed to be different. Embrace that. Being your authentic, God-made self naturally takes you where striving never could. But what about those areas in your life that you do want to change, like sin and struggle? That happens more naturally, too. I will explain in the next chapter.

QUESTIONS FOR PERSONAL REFLECTION

1. What gifts and abilities were you born with?
2. What spiritual gifts do you recognize you received with your salvation?
3. What have you considered to be some of the complications of your life, both in design and in circumstance?
4. How has God used your gifts and circumstances to guide your life so far?
5. Has this chapter led you to consider something about yourself you had not previously considered? How so?

Ending Your Battle with Sin

Put on your new nature, and be renewed as you
learn to know your Creator and become like
him. —Colossians 3:10

During a break at a conference, I overheard two attendees
discuss the last message presented. It was a teaching about
sin. I found the presentation insightful and refreshing. They
were not so sure. The color of their name tags told me that
they were church leaders of different generations. If I had
to guess, one was in his late thirties. The other was in his
low seventies. The question from the younger to the older
is what caught my attention.

"What did you think of the message?" The other guy
paused, folded his arms, and looked up to find the right words.
He bobbed his head from left to right and pursed his lips. It
took him about ten seconds to respond.

"I was really hoping to learn some methods for how to stop. . . ." He named a common vice like lust or pride. I tuned out shortly after. Not because I dismissed the man's feedback but because my mind started to race with thoughts.

The first one: *Stopping sin—isn't that what everyone is looking for?* Okay, maybe not everyone. But many think it is the quintessential goal of their Christian life. My inbox is filled with variations of the same question. "How do I stop being angry?" or "How do I stop overeating?" Some seek to break an addiction like smoking, drinking, or sex. These are not bad questions to ask.

My next thought: *What "method" has he not already heard?* The man had the vibe of an elder or a Sunday school teacher. I figured that he had sat through plenty of sin-management sermons in his day. He had probably read various books on the subject, too. There is no shortage of those. If a leader of his age and experience has not found the silver bullet to stop sin, maybe it is because there isn't one.

I contemplated that thought for the next week. It made me reflect on all the methods I had learned and tried. Scripture memorization. Fasting. More and different types of prayer. Accountability partners. Those are the usuals. But in desperation, people get creative. I know of teenagers who are taught to wear rubber bands to manage their impulses. When something impure crosses their minds, they are supposed to snap it against their wrist. In theory, the feeling of pain teaches them to stop the lust.

But that is only theory. Throughout history, people have subjected themselves to far more pain with nothing more than bruises and scars and poor health to show for it. Before he began the Protestant Reformation, Martin Luther, who lived in the sixteenth century, tried to purify himself through physical abuse. He struck his body frequently with a whip, and even slept naked in the snow.[1] Monks long before him went to greater lengths. Some fasted themselves to skin and bones. Men in one group each lived alone for years atop outdoor pillars.[2] None of it worked, which is why they kept trying.

Did the 1,500 years Israel spent trying to keep the Law not teach them anything? Has it not taught us anything? If pain, discipline, and devotion did not conquer sin back then, it will not today, no matter how much we modernize the methods or put a clever title on it. This does not mean that it is impossible to be better, though. It just means that it does not happen through a better method. We will get to what is most effective. The first step is to understand sin correctly.

The Real Meaning of Sin

How do you define sin? Think about that for a minute. If you grew up in church, you might say something like, "Sin is to miss the mark." Or "to fall short of God's best." Or "to willfully (or even accidentally) disobey God." None of those are incorrect. The Hebrew and Greek words for sin both mean to fail or miss the goal.[3]

Despite the general consensus in definition, whole denominations split and form over what is sin and what is not. Worse, people are derided, condemned, and iced out of families and friendships over it. The issue comes down to what is the standard, the goal, the mark—and how is it missed? Every Christian that I know cites the Bible to back up their ideas, as they should, of course.

Most begin with the Ten Commandments. Honesty is a standard. A day of rest is a standard. So is respect for your parents and faithfulness to your spouse. Obviously, do not murder, do not steal. There are many others mentioned in Scripture. Remember, the Ten Commandments are the first 10 of 613 laws that God gave Israel through Moses. People also esteem psalms, proverbs, and remarks made by the New Testament writers as God's standards, too. Sobriety is a good example. Purity is another one.

What gets crazy is when people classify sin as anything that might lead to failure. A joke I have heard among some former legalists illustrates this well. It begins with not standing up while doing something such as handholding or kissing. It ends with the punch line, "because it might lead to dancing." You are fortunate if you do not understand the humor of that phrase. It probably means that you were not raised to believe that dancing is a sin. But some people are. They are taught that since breaking purity is a sin, one must also avoid anything that might lead to it. The same is said about sobriety. Since alcohol can lead to drunkenness, some people command complete avoidance. I kid you not, some include the popular cold and flu medicine NyQuil. It contains ten percent alcohol.

The madness of this kind of logic is that there is no end to what could cause sin. It leads to goofy laws like the one I ridiculed in chapter 2. Do you remember the story of the lady whose church mandated that women may only wear pink or white fingernail polish? I am unsure what standard that helps to uphold. My best guess is the apostle Paul's encouragement to honor your body as God's temple (see 1 Corinthians 6:19–20). Maybe it is based on the 71st Law of

Moses: women must not wear men's clothes (see Deuteronomy 22:5). I scratch my head. It is the product of a poor interpretation, whatever it is. Or somebody's power trip.

But that is how it is with many of the so-called sins that people try desperately to avoid today. They are based on somebody's interpretation. Maybe an interpretation of an interpretation. Recall that this is what happened in Bible times, too. It is why Jesus invited people to "come to me, all of you who are weary and carry heavy burdens, and I will give you rest" (Matthew 11:28). The Mosaic Law was already impossible to follow, let alone the thousands of interpretations and precautions added by the religious leaders.

I do not mean to imply that everything is an interpretation. God has standards today. But you might be surprised to learn that they are not the Ten Commandments. Despite all the emphasis we give them these days, they are not a special set of laws. Paul referred to them as a part of "the old way . . . [that] led to death" (2 Corinthians 3:7). Coupled with the other 603 Laws of Moses, they revealed Israel's need for Jesus. To that end, they accomplished their purpose perfectly.

But that is the end of them (see Romans 10:4). If you do not accept that, then you must say goodbye to pulled pork sandwiches, Saturday yard work, shellfish, borrowing with interest, among many other things that you do or enjoy currently. When it comes to the Law, you cannot cherry pick what to follow. Scripture states clearly that when you break one of them, you are as guilty as if you had broken all of them (see James 2:10).

By fulfilling the Law, Jesus instituted the "new way" (2 Corinthians 3:9). It includes what you would expect that God desires, such as honesty, respect, and purity. It is the law of love. Love God. Love people. Jesus revealed this through everything He taught and did. Recall that in His Sermon on the Mount, He equated God's perfection with His unconditional love: "But you are to be perfect, even as your Father in heaven is perfect" (Matthew 5:48). In other words, love like God.

When a religious leader asked Him to name the most important commandment, Jesus responded, "Love the LORD your God . . . [and] love your neighbor as yourself" (Mark 12:29–31). Paul echoed the same. Throughout his letters, he maintained that God's standard is love (see Romans 13:8; Galatians 5:14). Jesus' beloved disciple, John, held to this, too. He said that obeying God comes down to faith in Jesus and love for one another (see 1 John 3:23).

On that point, John's words help to answer a question that I get frequently. People wonder how to explain all the New Testament references to obedience to God's commandments. Besides John's mention, there is Peter's exhortation to "be holy in everything you do" (1 Peter 1:15) and James' instruction to be doers of God's Word (see James 1:22). Perhaps most obvious, Jesus said, "If you love me, obey my commandments" (John 14:15). The solution to this supposed conundrum is simple. Read the context. It never refers to the Mosaic Law. In every case, it conveys just what John said. The commandment, the word, the demonstration of holiness always comes down to love.

What all of this means is that it is possible that your battle is not with real sin. It might be with a law that you are not meant to follow. It might be with someone's flawed interpretation, their paranoia, or their want for control. May you be freed! God's standard is straightforward and simple. It is love. Love God through your faith in Jesus. Then love people, which includes yourself. Having said that, what if your thoughts, words, or actions really do fall into the category of sin?

What to Really Stop

"Kyle, I have tried everything! I don't want to do this anymore!" a young man wrote. We will call him Garrett. His email was about pornography. I could sense his desperation by the amount of exclamation points he used. He shared how much he loves Jesus and how much he hates the addiction. I did not doubt that. Christians are not immune from struggle. Not even this one. It is called "the new drug" for how easily accessible and addictive it is.

I replied in the same way that I do to anyone who shares something like this with me. I told him that God loves him (which is very true) and that he is not alone in this battle (which is also very true—89 percent of Christian men and 51 percent of Christian women admit to it[4]). I also thanked him for trusting me enough to share. There is a great deal of shame associated with sexual struggle. It is a brave thing to let someone in on that kind of a secret. Before I made any suggestions, though, I asked what he meant by, "I have tried everything."

I could have predicted his response. Cold showers. Internet filters. Accountability partners. Self-deliverance books. Not bad things necessarily. Just a bunch of methods. He granted that each worked for a while. Still, there he was, emailing me, as addicted as before. Maybe more so, he worried. I could have predicted that, too. I proposed to him that his struggle may relate to the way he is trying to fight it. I find that to be the case for most of us. That is why I told him to stop the two counter-productive things that many Christians do to deal with sin.

Stop trying to stop.

It has been a while since chapter 2. We explored the reasons why regimens of restrictions are not effective. Biologically, our bodies act upon our thoughts. That means that you eventually do what is on your mind. Remember, this accounts for the failure of diets and drug programs. The spiritual principle behind this is that "law gives sin its power" (1 Corinthians 15:56). Any "must do" or "must not do" is a law. Focusing on them only leads to frustration, exhaustion, and more failure.

The apostle Paul explained this through his own experience. As a good Jew, he depended upon the Mosaic Law to conquer the sinful desires in him that it outlined. Naturally, some of the 613 commandments were easier for him to follow than others. The tenth commandment was not one of them. It instructs, "you must not covet" (Exodus 20:17). Paul had to work at that one. The problem is, the more that he tried to get it under control, the more that it controlled him. "Sin used this command to arouse all kinds of covetous desires within me" (Romans 7:8). Most of us can relate to what it perpetuated. "I want to do what is right, but I don't do it," he complained. "Instead, I do what I hate" (Romans 7:15).

Paul not only criticized dependance on Jewish Law, he condemned any kind of discipline to stop sin. He made that clear in his letter to the church at Colossae. You see, the

Colossian Christians lived in an especially sexualized culture. I imagine that their battles on that front were not all that different from ours, if not worse. People turned to a Greek method called *asceticism* to stop their desires. It demanded separation from anything that evoked pleasure.[5]

Paul saw this to be as dangerous as relying on the Law of Moses. He had to nip it in the bud quickly. "Why do you keep on following the rules of the world, such as 'Don't handle! Don't taste! Don't touch!'?" he asked as if they should know better. "These rules may seem wise because they require strong devotion, pious self-denial, and severe bodily discipline. But they provide no help in conquering a person's evil desires" (Colossians 2:21–23).

No help. Whether a Ten Commandment or some contemporary self-help principle, Paul maintained that depending on any rule or discipline to stop sin is a waste of effort at best. But it may even enslave you further. That was Garrett's experience. All his effort and methods did not stop the bad behavior. They just produced guilt, which influenced more bad behavior. That brought me to my second suggestion.

Stop feeling bad about yourself.

Failure usually results in feelings of guilt and shame. Many not only hate what they did (guilt), but they hate themselves for it (shame). From our back-and-forth email exchange, I could tell that this was no different for Garrett. He loathed himself, which came naturally. But he was also told that God wanted him to feel bad, too.

I hear this a lot. Especially from those steeped in religion. Some traditions celebrate guilt and shame, and even suggest ways to provoke these feelings. In childhood, I was part of one that did. After we confessed our failures, the priest sent us away with "homework" to emphasize the weight of our mistakes. They called it a penance. The idea, as I understood it, is that a sense of guilt and punishment motivates you to do better in the future. It reminds me of the potty-training technique that I came across during the two months that I had a puppy. Some suggest that rubbing a dog's nose in their accident trains them to have fewer accidents. I did not try this. Newer research shows that it backfires in a huge way. It only teaches the dog to fear its owner or hide its mistakes.

Does shame not do the same to humans? Isn't this the story of Adam and Eve? After their failure, they felt ashamed. That did not produce anything beneficial. It only led them to hide from God. What human since the first couple can honestly claim that shame has resulted in any other experience? Who has really become better by wallowing in grief because he or she failed? I have not met anyone who can say so without crossing their fingers behind their back.

Sure, they might want to believe so. Like a dog who learns to hide his mistakes out of fear, they might try to dress themselves up to look so. But the truth is, feeling like a failure—what Paul called "worldly sorrow"—only fuels failure (see 2 Corinthians 7:10). This does not mean you should be callous about failure, of course. Just do not believe that you must pay for it with bad thoughts or feelings about yourself. Or with anything at all. As the author of Hebrews said, guilt that is accompanied with some sort of burden to pay or be punished keeps people conscious of sin. And that leads to more sin (see Hebrews 10:2–3). In other words, if you fixate on how bad you are, your bad feelings will drive you to do bad things. Another product of the mind's puppetry over the flesh.

After I shared this idea with Garrett, I concluded lovingly, "Your focus is all wrong." He was stuck in sin because his mind was stuck on sin. I assured him that though perfection is not the goal, God does not desire for him to be enslaved to this addiction, or any other kind of harmful behavior.

It is the same for you. Though God does not expect you to be perfect, nor do your behaviors change His mind about you, He does care about them. God is not apathetic to your struggles. But dos and don'ts do not produce good behavior. Nor does self-loathing motivate anyone to do better. It never has. It never will. As I later explained to Garrett, good beliefs produce good behavior. Particularly, beliefs about who you are and what you have because of God's grace.

The Power of Grace-Based Beliefs

Grace gets a bad rap for being light on sin. Some people think that the idea of being forgiven forever means that Christians will follow their every impulse right into the gutter. And some do find themselves in the gutter, I guess. Some email me from the gutter. But that is because we are human, not because we feel allowed to sin or even want to sin. I do not know a Christian who *wants* to fail. Do you want to fail? Of course not. Like Garrett and others who contact me, you hate to fail, even though you still do at times. I know that. God knows that. He said it Himself: "The spirit is willing, but the body is weak" (Matthew 26:41).

Be that as it may, despite the theories of legalists, knowing that you remain forgiven actually helps you sin less. As I have said all throughout this book, when you know that nothing is on the line, you do better. Still, there is far more to grace than forgiveness. It is also about who you are and what you have in Christ. Knowing that especially helps you sin less.

Dr. Andrew Farley and I discussed this on my podcast. He is one of today's great minds on grace. While on the topic of sin, he offered an enlightening illustration using the state of a house he once owned. "I lived in a house that had three bedrooms. One of those bedrooms was our master, but the other two were, one was for a guest, and then one was my office." He confessed that his office was filthy, a wreck. But the guest room was pristine. "Imagine you're walking down the hallway of that house with a piece of garbage all balled up ready to toss somewhere. Where are you going to toss it? Are you going to toss it in the clean guest room or my office?"[6] The obvious answer is the dirty one. He explained that since you already consider it dirty, adding another piece of garbage is usually not a problem.

That's brilliant, I thought as I glanced at my junk drawer across the room. Who does not have one of those? Since you already defined it as a place for junk, you do not mind adding more junk to it. Am I right? But are you as likely to add the wrinkled receipt or the promotional pen or the loose change to the (hopefully) clean utensil drawer? Probably not. The point is, whether it is a room, a drawer, or you, you are more likely to keep clean what you see as clean. So, see yourself as clean! Because you are! As a result, you will naturally live a cleaner life.

Think of it this way: right believing influences right behaving, which results in right living. This could sound like modern psychology. And while, yes, psychology understands the principle of being positive, this field did not invent the principle. Again, God designed the mind to influence the body. Positivity is His idea.

Besides, this is not about thinking, "I can, I can, I can." This is about simply accepting the truth of who you are as a new person in Christ. That is what the apostle Paul taught on this very subject. To beat vices such as lust, lies, and anger, he instructed, "Put on your new nature, created to be like God—truly righteous and holy" (Ephesians 4:24). I once believed this was some kind of method of behavior modification. "Put on" sounded like a routine or a ritual. It isn't. "Put on" is from a Greek concept that means to see yourself as having a certain quality or character.[7]

In other words, accept it and identify with it. Take it as yours. Forget the lie that you are a horrible sinner and accept the truth that in Christ you are new, right, whole, and holy. That is your best chance to sin less.

Sinning less, of course, is a good desire for many reasons. Sin can hurt you; it can hurt others; it can hurt your love for God. Like I said, God cares about all of that. But if the Bible is right in that God does not count our sins against us anymore, then overcoming sin is not the ultimate goal of the Christian life. In the next chapter, we will explore the most empowering truth that I learned the hard way.

QUESTIONS FOR PERSONAL REFLECTION

1. Has your Christian life been centered around managing sin? How has this helped or hindered your relationship with God?

2. What methods have you used to manage sin? What were the results?

3. When you fail, what is the first thing you feel and think? How does that affect your behavior?

4. Consider the battles that you have faced or are facing currently. Would you classify them under the Law of Moses, someone else's law, or the law of love?

5. After reading this chapter, how will you address (real) sin more effectively?

11

The Ground of Growth

Your roots will grow down into God's love and keep you strong.   —Ephesians 3:17

I had not stood on the platform of my high school youth group for eighteen years. A whole lot of life had happened since that speaking opportunity my first summer home from college. No longer a kid, not really an adult. Somewhere in the undefinable in-between. Still wet behind the ears, as my grandma used to say.

I guess they saw something in me, though. By the end of the summer, the leadership invited me to speak. I do not recall anyone else my age having that opportunity. I had them fooled. By the age of nineteen, I had mastered the art of wearing a mask. It was a survival technique that I had developed to get through school. A façade of confidence guarded an internal garden of insecurity and shame—a garden from which I often picked and ate of its fruit when no one was looking. They were unaware that it was this garden that had prompted my leap toward faith a few years earlier. My hope was that it could uproot the wrongness that I had felt for as long as I can remember. Nothing else had worked. I figured Jesus could do it. And He did. Just very differently from how I thought He would. But that is getting ahead of myself.

I only remember two things about the message I gave that summer: its title was "Purpose or Distractions," and I could not get the bat on the ball. This was back before cell phone cameras and YouTube, thankfully. It forever remains only in the minds of those who endured it. All of whom have undoubtedly forgotten it. It took me a while to forget it, though. My façade of confidence was built with the bricks of atta-boys and accolades. The lack of those after the message reinforced the feeling of failure that arose in me halfway through it. This provided a feast of fruit for weeks, maybe months, later.

Like I said, a lot had happened since then. When I was asked to return to the same platform to address a youth lock-in, I was well established in ministry. I had spoken in churches across the country. I had three books under my belt and a slew of media appearances. Nonetheless, I wondered if the outcome would be any different. Not for the same reasons. I have learned how to craft a message. But could I craft one that relates to a TikTok generation that has a few-second attention span?

After weeks of prayer and reflection, I realized what I needed to say. But it was not something trivial or light-hearted. Not the stereotypical youth-group message, that's for sure. It would be revelation for most adults. I wondered if freshmen in high school could comprehend it, much less appreciate it? I knew it would be a gamble. Still, I had to tell them that for many years I misunderstood the goal of the Christian life.

The Goal of the Christian Life

Besides a wall that had been removed, not much else had changed in almost two decades. The carpet. The chairs. Even the five-foot metal giraffe that we splurged to buy on an outing. Seeing that still in the corner of the room really took me back. I remembered the store in which we found it. The price. And the excitement. For some reason it seemed the perfect complement to our newly constructed space.

After a bit of time with the kids, I realized that not much had changed with teenagers, either. Sure, their clothes were different. (Tighter than they were in my day.) Hairstyles had certainly changed. Their lingo, too. But on some of them I recognized the same façade of confidence that I had hidden behind at their age. I heard the same insecurity in their voices. I saw the same fear in their eyes. As they worshipped later, a few exhibited the same unmistakable posture of desperation. The hope of change. I can spot that anywhere.

It was my turn to speak. I began with the story of how I ended up at the church at sixteen years old. I shared how I felt after my first visit. "I fell in love with Jesus when I heard how much He loved me," I said. "I had hope for the first time in my life that things could be different." Then I explained how somewhere along the way something had changed. "I went down the slippery slope of religion. I made the faith about proving myself to God. How much better I could be. How much less I could sin." Seeing their thumbs twiddling as they stared at the floor, I knew they understood.

"I became so performance focused," I confessed, "that I disregarded the simple message of God's love as spiritual baby food that Christians need to get beyond." That is no exaggeration. I am embarrassed to say that in college I used to complain when I heard that the weekend message would be about God's love. "Can't we get on to something deeper?" I grumbled to friends. I thought that people would benefit more from learning about spiritual disciplines and being led into spiritual experiences. In hindsight, I suppose that is because I believed *I* would benefit more from them. Isn't that how it is? We think everyone else needs what we need.

It took me a decade of hard-learned lessons to realize that is not what I needed. "Despite everything I did and achieved, I still felt lacking," I told them. "I still felt I was disappointing to God. Still wrong. Still shameful. Not much different than when I sat in this very room as a teenager." I think they were surprised to hear this. Many of their parents had watched my path to ministry. I was one of their success stories. Some of the teens knew that. But I did not want my put-together persona to fool them. I let them in on some things that they did not know: the years of tears that I shed in private from the *God-can't-use-you* accusations that reverberated in my head; the rejection triggers that I wrestled down more often than I cared to admit; how the reality of past regrets and present imperfections once had me *this close* to abandoning my call.

"But I stand here a changed man," I insisted. "All of the frustration that came from years of trying to improve myself drove me to the only thing that matters." I paused for a few seconds to build some tension. That is another preacher trick. But I also did not want them to miss what I was about to say. It was this: "The Christian life is not about being better. The Christian life is about being loved."

I know that to make such a claim, I better have Bible verses to back it up, even in a youth message. I took them to a passage that is known as "Paul's Prayer for Spiritual Growth." He wrote it from prison to the church at Ephesus. I guess, even for Paul, there is something about rock bottom that reveals what matters most. He did not challenge them with something more to do. He pointed them to God's love. He implored them to search the depths and width and height of it and ground themselves in it. "May you experience the love of Christ," he prayed. "Then you will be made complete with all the fullness of life and power that comes from God" (Ephesians 3:19).

So much for the message of God's love being something to grow out of. According to Paul, it is the thing to grow into and the thing we grow from. It is the source of all strength, wholeness, and power. As I told the youth group, I found it to be the thread of my worth, the ground of my growth. During the remaining twenty or so minutes, I touched on some of what love produces that no amount of discipline, devotion, or willpower can. But a single message can only go so deep these days, especially one to a teenage audience. My opportunity for depth came a few months later over a long dinner.

The Big Change

I felt the vibration against my leg from an incoming text message. I pulled my phone out of my pocket to see, "Hey buddy! I'm in town this week. Any chance we can meet up?" It was from a former co-worker. A friend, really. We had worked together closely in ministry for about five years. But that had been a decade before this text message. Since then, I had launched my own ministry and moved hours away.

I readily admit that it is difficult for me to keep in touch with people who do not live nearby. As an introvert, communication exhausts me. It is almost as if I begin each day with a talk-tank that gets depleted by about four or five in the afternoon, and that might be stretching it. It is nothing personal, but one of the last things I want to do is spend an evening on the phone. I prefer to spend it a few miles down the road at Walt Disney World people watching. I wish I was joking; I do. But it is just one of the many parts of me that I no longer try to fix.

What all this means is that my friend and I had not had an in-depth conversation in a while. Though I would have to forgo Disney for an evening, I figured it would be nice to catch up over dinner while he was in town. We met at a bar and grill. And this time, I did not throw a single stink eye at those enjoying happy-hour drinks. That was markedly different than a decade earlier.

I do not remember how he and I got on the subject. Maybe it had something to do with the couple at the table next to us. Or maybe it was because we were across the street from a college campus. Whatever the impetus, somehow our conversation turned to God's love and grace. And somehow it felt as if my talk-tank was refilled. Somewhere toward the beginning of our conversation I told him that I no longer try to change people's behavior. He was surprised to hear this, especially from a ministry leader.

"Isn't that the whole point of ministry?" he asked. "If you don't instruct people about how to live better, then what do you say?"

A smile spread across my face as I remarked, "God loves you!"

He looked bewildered and waited for more. I reminded him of the apostle Paul's assurance that God's kindness leads people to repentance (see Romans 2:4). He knew that verse, of course.

"But don't you need to warn people about sin?" he pressed. "Don't you need to teach them what God expects?" To be sure, he was not combative. He was genuinely interested to learn.

I got theological. I explained that Jesus taught that the Holy Spirit convicts those in the world of their unbelief, not of their every sin (see John 16:8–9). I shared that as Jesus' representative, the Spirit does it as Jesus did, which is through love.

"If the Holy Spirit uses that approach, shouldn't we?" I asked.

His eyes shot up, then left, then right, then back up, as he considered what I said. "But what about for believers?"

"It's not really any different," I answered. I explained that the Holy Spirit is our advocate (see Romans 3:25–28). He is with us to remind us of God's grace. I sprinkled in a few verses from Paul about how "we are made right with God by placing our faith in Jesus" (Romans 3:22). By this time, we had finished our meals, but I offered some food for thought: "How much better can someone get than made right?"

I could almost hear his wheels spinning in the silence, which I broke with a clarification. "Of course, Christians change and grow and mature," I assured. "And yes, God desires for our lives to become more Christlike. We should want that, too. I just find that all happens naturally when people know that they are loved."

I knew instantly that I had backed myself into a corner with that statement. He confirmed as much when he crossed his arms while leaning back in his chair. I had to make a quick decision. I could cite more Bible verses. I could even offer science about how a sense of love reduces the stress hormone that leads to failure. Or I could teach him how studies find that love promotes good health and healing.[1] *But that is all theory*, I reasoned to myself. It was time to get personal. I asked him to recall what I had pursued when we worked together, besides the newer technology or the nicer car.

"Supernatural experiences," he replied without hesitation. That is what I hoped he would say. In those days, I chased all the sensational stuff. I believed that there is nothing a good Holy Ghost meeting could not solve. Nothing wrong with those, by the way. I still enjoy them, just not for the same reasons.

"I pursued all of that back then with the hope that they would fix me," I revealed to him. Not like an addiction or a symptom. But *me*. I had his attention. He leaned in, allowed me to go on. "All the laying on of hands didn't impart a better version of *me*. Another prophetic word didn't change my insecurity about *me*. No deliverance prayer ever rid me of *me*." Then I told him what I had told the teenagers a few months earlier at the lock-in: "Nothing changed me like resting in the realization that God loves me . . . *just as I am*." He said he had a hundred questions, but first, he needed me to clarify "just as I am." He feared that might mean a license to sin.

The License of Love

That again, I thought just a split second before I retorted abruptly, "Nobody needs a license to sin; we sin just fine without one." I did not mean to be so snarky. It is just that the license-to-sin line gets old.

But I get it. That was once my go-to line, too. I believed that unconditional love might encourage unlimited sin. As I said in the last chapter, it doesn't. But it does allow for sin, which we better thank God that it does. Otherwise, we are all in trouble. Because who can honestly claim to be free of sin? Sure, perhaps you are innocent of the big stuff. Murder, adultery, theft, and the like. Yes, those have more serious natural consequences than, say, a lie. Scripturally, though, sin is sin is sin. None of us are free of it. As Paul reminded, "We all fall short of God's glorious standard" (Romans 3:23). Every single day.

Having explained that, I regained my composure and added, "While I don't know a Christian that truly *wants* a license to sin, I do know many who need a license to be loved." A decade of receiving prayer requests has convinced me of this. Almost everyone knows that love is one of God's qualities. And apart from some angry sign-wavers, most do not find it difficult to say, "God loves you." But few can say, "God loves me" and really mean it, especially on their bad days.

Without exception, this is a trait that I have observed in struggling people. It does not matter where it lies on the spectrum between sex addiction, substance abuse, or perfectionism, most toxic behavior is either a means to ease the pain of feeling unloved or an effort to earn love. I guess it takes one to know one. I never traveled the path to sex, drugs, or alcohol, fortunately. But perfectionism? Absolutely. An obsession with achievement? You bet. These were responses to shame, ways to earn and feel love.

My friend understood that well enough. Most people do. The pursuit of love might be the most universal human thing. But he wanted to get back to the change that I had experienced.

"How does God's love help you to please God?" he asked. I decided not to debate the semantics of his question. It took me the good part of a decade to grasp that in Christ we are as pleasing to God as we can get. Besides, I knew what he meant. He wanted me to show the receipts of the effortless growth that I claimed to have experienced.

We were two hours into our dinner at this point. Taking a bathroom break, he challenged, "Use this time to think of your best answer." I did not need the time, though. In fact, I grew impatient waiting for him to return to the table. It was like fire shut up in my bones. Just as soon as he sat down again, I beamed, "God's love freed me to be me!"

Free to Be Me

In elementary school, I continued to do something that hurt my mother deeply. I did not mean to do it, but at the same time, I could not tell her why I did it: I never invited her to class parties or parent days. Sometimes I downright lied to her about them so that she did not show up. (That did not stop her or my dad.) Naturally, she took my behavior as rejection. She believed that I was ashamed of her. What I wanted to tell her so badly back then but could not is that my behavior had nothing to do with her. I was ashamed of *me*. The last thing I wanted anyone to see was me at school sitting or playing alone without any friends. I kept that guarded behind my façade until my upper twenties. It was through a TV interview, of all things, that she finally heard the truth.

You see, I was embarrassed of myself for so long. That might be putting it too lightly. In many ways, I hated myself. This is why I learned to wear a mask so well. During childhood, I came to believe that the most authentic parts of me were unlovable or unacceptable. My quiet personality. My preference for art class over physical education class. My inability to pass a ball. Even my love for country music (I know, I know).

It seemed that everything about me made me an outcast, different. Probably because it kept being reinforced with name calling and rejection. In my freshman year, some guys taped a newspaper clipping of me being featured as a "scholar of the week" above the locker room door. If I remember correctly, they wrote some humiliating words over my forehead. Why? They didn't like *me*. Something was wrong with *me* . . . yet again.

I find it hard to put into words. But something tells me that you will understand what I mean. Even though I did not choose how people treated me, I still felt ashamed by it. That is the crazy thing about any level of trauma, and mine is child's play compared to what others have experienced. Somehow, someone else's wrong is *my* wrong. You fear what people will think about you if they know it. I did. I kept it all a secret even to someone as close as my mom.

But secrets make you sick. And sickness leads to medicine (or coping mechanisms or escapism). As I said, my "medicine" was perfectionism, achievement, and even religion. I worked them as much as I could, until I found that while they can hide things, they cannot heal things. This culminated in my "What more do I need to do, God?" question. His answer was for me to accept His love. Simple as that, though maybe not as overnight as it sounds. It was a journey.

Face-to-face with the finished work of the cross on my apartment floor was the kick starter. Then came years of unlearning lies and accepting certain truths (more on that in the next chapter). Sure enough, though, just as Paul assured, my strength and wholeness came naturally as I grew in my understanding of God's love (see Ephesians 3:17–19). Then one day there I was, in front of a camera, sharing some of my secrets on TV. And now in this book.

How does that work exactly? I don't know. But it seems that a good deal of love's power is in what it does to fear. "Perfect love expels all fear" (1 John 4:18). As I said earlier in the book, John did not really mean fear of spiders, heights, or public speaking. He meant that love ousts the worry that you are bad and that God is mad, which is shame. God's love allows you to embrace the qualities about yourself that you fear, maybe hate. It heals the parts of your story that you are afraid to admit, much less share. It is not that it erases your memory or makes you deny that something exists. You just know that none of it defines you anymore. Growth is exponential from there. With no shame associated with those things you once feared were wrong about you, God gets to use you as He made you for the reasons for which He made you.

If you want to talk about a crucified life, this is it. Accepting that you are loved unconditionally takes the focus off your instinct for self-preservation and people pleasing. At least enough to say as the prophet Isaiah said, "Here I am [Lord]. Send me" (Isaiah 6:8). Imperfections and all.

In fact, it makes it empowering to be sent and seen as you are. Because when you know that you are loved without exception, you somehow find that your imperfections are your unfair advantage. Nothing demonstrates God's power as they do. Nothing helps others relate to you as they do. I found ministry in that. You will find there is no greater satisfaction than that. In so many words, I explained all of this to my friend at dinner. He sat there, wide-eyed, taking it all in.

"Everything that God desires—His law of love—is both empowered and fulfilled by His love," I boasted. "You'll never love God more than when you accept His unconditional love. You'll never trust Him more than when you accept His unconditional love. And you'll never love others more than when you accept His unconditional love." That brought me to my next big change.

The Power to Love

When it comes to loving people, Jesus instructed, "Love your neighbor as yourself" (Matthew 22:39). Legalists usually balk when someone suggests that this means you must love yourself first. They claim that is not what Jesus meant. And this might be one of the few times that I agree with them, technically. I know that Jesus' words mean to love others as if they are you. That is, since you would not hurt yourself, you should not hurt others. Since you would not curse yourself, you should not curse others. You get the point.

But who can deny the wisdom that to be able to love others, you have to love yourself first? As it is said so often, you cannot give something that you do not have. Common sense does not require a Bible verse. Yet the idea is rooted in Scripture. After

John wrote that "perfect love expels all fear," he added, "We love each other because he loved us first" (1 John 4:18–19). Do you recognize the progression in that? Only by receiving God's love for you can you give His love to others.

Many people are surprised to learn that in my first decade of faith, I had little compassion. They figure that someone as wounded as I was would naturally feel for others. Empathy is the word for it. That might be true for some. But for others like me, hurting people hurt people. Not always physically, of course. I did not harm people. But I was hard on people through my words and advice. Definitely in my thoughts. Good thing nobody could see those! I had no grace for failure. No mercy for mistakes. Self-righteousness is all I had to give. Pressed down. Shaken together. And running over!

Accepting God's unconditional love changed this about me. I have friends who have feared that it changed it too much. They have misinterpreted my consideration for people as condoning everything. That's not it at all. It is just that I have learned that there is no opportunity for ministry in condemnation. And a list of things to fix fixes nothing. Mostly, though, the more I know God's love through my imperfections and differences, the more compassion I have for the imperfections and differences of others, whatever they might be. And therein is a secret to loving others.

That is also a secret to my walks at Disney World. Since it is one of the world's most visited destinations, you encounter people there from every walk of life. You stand next to them for an hour or two in line waiting for an attraction. You rub shoulders with them during the fireworks show. They run over your toes with their strollers in the mad rush out. It is a legalist's nightmare. Anyway, I do not claim that my thoughts about people are perfect. I sometimes still think, *Why are you like that?* But even that question shows my progress. Because I *wonder* why; I don't *assume* why.

As Paul said, "Love is patient and kind. Love is not jealous or boastful or proud or rude" (1 Corinthians 13:4–5). In other words, it does not rush to judgment, but it takes the time to understand with humility. Among many other demonstrations, love takes that weird walking (or talking or looking or believing or living) person to lunch and says, "I know I am meeting you in your seventh chapter. Tell me about chapters one through six." And then it listens. Not to offer a fix-it solution. It listens for the opportunity to say, "God loves you." And then maybe, if God wills, it gives you the opportunity to walk with them in their weird kind of walk. If you want to talk about Christlikeness, show me something that looks more like Jesus.

Are you surprised to hear that our dinnertime catch-up went on for four hours? I do not know if my friend agreed with all my conclusions. But he could not disagree that I had changed in the decade since we had worked together. That's the power of love. I finished my conversation with him the same way I finished it with the teenagers at the lock-in. I say the same to you: Be you, and be loved. That's all, but that's everything. Next, let's talk more practically about how to accept that.

QUESTIONS FOR PERSONAL REFLECTION

1. Up until now, what all have you done to pursue healing, growth, and Christlikeness?

2. What aspects of your life have kept you from accepting that God loves you as you are?

3. How have you tried to hide or heal the qualities that you dislike about yourself?

4. In what ways could accepting God's unconditional love free you?

5. How might accepting God's unconditional love for you affect the way you think about or relate with other people?

12

How to Accept God's Love

For we know how dearly God loves us, because he has given us the Holy Spirit to fill our hearts with his love. —Romans 5:5

"How?" appeared at the top-right of my screen shortly after I ended my webcast. It was the subject of an email from a lady named Rachel. My story of God's love convinced her that she needed to experience it for herself. But she did not know how.

Rachel was not a new Christian. She was in her mid-thirties when she wrote me. Growing up in a church-going family, she gave her life to Jesus at the age of nine, was baptized almost immediately after, and received the right hand of fellowship while still drying off (her church's phrase for membership). While that is when she considers herself saved, she cannot remember a time when she did not believe in Jesus. I can relate. My parents have recorded my very first phrase as "pray Jesus." My mom is convinced that was prophetic of my future. I don't know. It may have only been the result of Dad's insistence that we never miss a Sunday obligation (their church's phrase for "it's a sin to miss church"). Undoubtedly, what I heard week in and week out shaped my toddler mind. While I say I came to faith in Jesus at sixteen years old, I cannot remember never believing in Him, either.

Believing in God and believing that He loves you, however, are two very different things. Our seemingly model Christian upbringings worked well for the believing-in-God part. Yet somehow, despite relentless church attendance, we both missed the love part. As I said earlier in this book, that is more common than not. There are many reasons for it. I am not here to point fingers, though, except at the enemy who works to blind our minds to it (see 2 Corinthians 4:4). Rachel went on to explain that she has no problem accepting that God loves others. "But how do I truly accept His love for myself?"

What a question, I thought. The effects of God's love are easy to describe. Just like it is easy to describe the effects of gravity. I can say that I am able to stand today because of both. But like gravity, God's love is an invisible and intangible force. How do you instruct someone to accept something that they cannot put their hands on physically? Where do you begin? Do you advise them to sit cross-legged on the floor, close their eyes, extend their open palms toward the heavens, and breathe deeply? Then what?

Rachel would not be the last person to ask me this question. But she was the first. And honestly, it caught me off guard. I had to do some thinking and retrace my journey.

I never sat cross-legged on the floor with extended hands. Yes, I have had experiences that showed me God's love. They personalized things that Scripture already revealed. That I am worthy of love. And the loving lengths God went for me. Those are monumental revelations, of course. But through what process did those revelations make their way from my head to my heart so that I felt loved?

After considering the question for a while, I realized I had it backward. Accepting God's love was not about getting it from my head to my heart. It was about getting what is in my heart into my head. You see, the Bible assures that God poured His love into our hearts (see Romans 5:5). You are loved whether you know it or not. You are loved whether you feel it or not. But for it to really affect you, you must believe it. How you talk, walk, and live is influenced by what you believe.

It was not an overnight thing for me to get here. The path from my heart to my head was blocked by a lifetime of lies, each of which had to be replaced with certain truths. I have found that is the case for everyone who struggles to accept that they are loved. It takes a reprogramming of the mind, which takes time—there is no way around it. Nevertheless, I am here to help shorten that time for you with some truths that helped me. The first one has to do with your secrets.

Truth #1: You Are Fully Known and Fully Loved

Sad to say, it took nearly thirty years for me to feel loved. That is not from a lack of people who loved me. My parents were not only insistent about church attendance, but they were also insistent about attending to the lives of my brothers and me. Were they perfect? That goes without saying. But I know they did the best they could with what they had, with what they knew.

The issue is that I did not believe in the love I was given because I did not feel truly known. Whether from my parents or friends, I disregarded any mention or gesture of love with a thought like, "You would not love me if you really knew me." Not that I helped anyone get to know me. No way! I built walls to keep people far from the threshold of my secrets. Far from the chance to be utterly rejected. Far from the chance to be deemed a creature with five heads, seven eyes, warts, and a stench. Shame exaggerates things like that. It uses darkness to turn a tinker toy into a monster who lurks in the corner of the room.

Then one day, while I was in my room, God shined a light that helped me come out from under the cover of fear. It was a light into His Word. I did not go looking for it. But that is how God's revelations work, I suppose. They just show up when you need them. And boy did I need this one. After my regular ritual of apologizing for myself to God, my eyes caught an open page of the Bible that was in my hands. "Even before he made the world, God loved us and chose us in Christ to be holy and without fault in his eyes" (Ephesians 1:4). This was not a new verse to me. Yet it felt entirely new when I heard God say, *You are no surprise to me. I knew all of that when I made you, yet I still made you. And I still love you.*

Allow me to clarify what I mean by "say." Except for one iffy dream that I had as a teenager in which God rang me on my cell phone, I have never heard the audible voice of God. He usually speaks to me through the voice of Scripture or a random thought that enters my mind. This was one of those moments. I do not believe I produced the thought myself, but even if so, it does not contradict the verse. The verse clearly says that God knew each of us before He made us. *Everything* about us. The good, the bad, and the ugly. Yet He still brought us into existence. And He still loves us.

Isn't this what King David knew, too? Recall his psalm that we explored in chapter 9. He prayed, "O Lord, you have examined my heart and know everything about me" (Psalm 139:1). Indeed, as David continued to detail, that included the basic contours of his life, when he sits and stands, when he travels and rests. But he also understood that God is present for his every deed and aware of his every thought. For most of my life, that idea frightened me. I did not want to think about what all God had seen and heard.

If anyone should have felt that fear, David should have. For one, he committed adultery with Bathsheba, then plotted to have her husband killed. Even the thoughts that lead to such acts are scandalous enough, let alone the acts themselves. Yet David praised God for His knowledge and even invited Him further into His thoughts (see verses 23–24).

Knowing that God knew such dreadful things about him, how could David maintain such intimacy and confidence with Him? He knew that he was unconditionally loved, that's how (see Psalm 138:8). He was certain that God had good and precious thoughts about him (see Psalm 139:17). He felt safe in a relationship with a God he knew would never forsake him, never throw him away, not for anything (see verses 7–11).

Amazingly, David was sure of all this long before the fullness of God's character was unveiled through Jesus. Now that the cross has rendered our secrets meaningless and us righteous, how much more should we feel safe with God? Infinitely more, I say. There is no chance of that changing.

As soon as I realized this truth, I was able to let love in—after almost thirty years. First and foremost, from God. Then, in time, from some of His people, too. That is because accepting God's love removes the shame, which then allows you to take down your walls to let some trusted people see into the real you. The feeling—and healing—of love compounds from there, I promise.

I also promise that it is true that you only feel as loved as you feel that you are known. With God, you have as much of both as you can get. Knowing all about you, God loved you first. Knowing the most about you, God loves you most. And no matter what you do in the future, God will always love you. If you still find it difficult to accept this truth, the next two will help.

Truth #2: You Cannot Disappoint God

I have not yet met a Christian who does not believe that God is all knowing ("omniscient," for the theologically astute). I have met plenty who do not live as if He knows everything, though. Much of our stress and striving are rooted in that. Mine were. By not studying hard enough, attending enough church functions, or talking to enough people about Jesus, I feared I would let down God, which would affect His opinion of me. I even felt guilty about taking afternoon naps. I worried He might see me as lazy. Or that I might miss something in even a sliver of downtime that jeopardized His plans for me.

Speaking of naps, I know that the psalmist says that God never slumbers or sleeps (see Psalm 121:4). But for the sake of argument, let's pretend He takes naps. God's omniscience means that He will never awake to find that you are not what He had hoped. Leaving aside the idea of God "waking up," how could He? Remember, God knew you before you were born, and watched as you were woven together in your mother's womb (see Psalm 139:15).

This means that there is zero chance that something about you takes Him off guard. He did not have to wait for your parents' gender reveal party to know what you would be. He was not shocked to discover the color of your hair. He was not surprised to know that you have ADHD or that you struggle with having too many Krispy Kreme donuts. He is not stunned that you are an introvert instead of an extrovert, or vice versa. Since nothing can take Him off guard, nothing can disappoint Him.

Somebody on social media tried to argue with me about that. (These people sure do provide plenty of content.) As far as they were concerned, God is always disappointed. "Look at the state of the world," they said. "How can He not be?" This was an instance when I could not help but respond. Trying my best to love like Jesus, I referred them to the definition of "disappointed." I even Googled it for them. (How is that for kind?) It means, "sad or displeased because someone has failed to fulfill one's expectations."[1] I followed my loving gesture with a simple question: If God is all-knowing, how can He be let down by expectations? They hemmed and hawed and countered with a few Bible verses.

I admit that I do not understand everything about God's omniscience and our free choice. Mystery is the only conclusion we can come to about some things. I am satisfied with that. The stories of God's people in Scripture, however, do not leave much mystery when it comes to what He knew about them. God chose Moses to lead His people out of slavery to the Egyptians. He was not disappointed to hear that Moses had a speech impediment. Later, God chose Gideon to deliver His people from the terror of the Midianites. He was not disappointed to find Gideon in a cave, hiding from them. He was not let down to see Gideon's insecurity. God's only response was to say, "Go with the strength you have . . . I am sending you" (Judges 6:14). As with Moses, God had already accounted for his weaknesses. They were all baked into the plan. As are yours. You cannot be a disappointment to God. You cannot behave in a way that disappoints Him, either.

The apostle Peter's story is a New Testament example of both. Jesus found him exhausted and no doubt irritable after a failed night of fishing. Yet He urged him to give it one more shot. "Go out where it is deeper, and let down your nets to catch some fish," Jesus directed (Luke 5:4). Peter grumbled at first. The nets were already cleaned. And they were heavy. Casting them out again was no small effort. Even so, he relented.

As the story goes, the nets filled with fish almost instantly. And almost just as instantly, Peter fell to his knees, begging, "Oh, Lord, please leave me—I'm such a sinful man" (verse 8). Jesus did not have to tap into His supernatural intuition to know this. Fishermen were a rough class of people. The job demanded a high level of labor, which attracted men not known for stellar attitudes. Nor child-friendly language.[2]

Peter saw himself as totally unworthy. Jesus did not comment on that. Instead, He spoke peace and destiny to him. "Don't be afraid! From now on you'll be fishing for people!" (verse 10). Jesus would later explain it with more detail. "You are Peter (which means 'rock'), and upon this rock I will build my church" (Matthew 16:18). Did Peter comprehend what any of that meant? It does not appear that way. It also does not appear that he had any clue as to how to accomplish it.

From the moment Peter left the shore, he stumbled his way to his destiny. He misinterpreted and misunderstood parables. When he tried to walk on water with Jesus, he lost faith and sank. When he was supposed to keep watch while Jesus prayed in the Garden of Gethsemane, he fell asleep. After Jesus' arrest, Peter denied knowing Him. The list of his failures is long. The denials, though, devastated him (see Matthew 26:75). But was Jesus devastated? Did Jesus discover something new about Peter? Something that led Him to believe He had chosen the wrong person? Something that caused Him to cancel His plans for Peter?

After His resurrection, Jesus found Peter back where it all began—along the shore, humbled from another failed night of fishing. Jesus did not take the opportunity to kick him while he was down. There was no, "How could you?" or "I told you so." That is not Jesus' operating style. He took Peter aside, then asked him, "Do you love me?"

"Yes, Lord," Peter replied, "you know I love you."

"Then feed my lambs," Jesus told him.

Jesus asked again. Same response.

"Then take care of my sheep."

Jesus asked a third time, "Do you love me?"

"Lord, you know everything. You know that I love you."

Jesus said, "Then feed my sheep" (see John 21:15–17).

Scholars, doing what scholars do, debate the meaning of this interaction. As with anything God does, its significance is layered, I am sure. But it cannot be coincidence that Jesus met Peter at the place of His calling and reaffirmed it, once for each denial he made. Through this, Jesus again spoke peace and destiny to Peter's sense of unworthiness. The way I see it, Jesus said, "I know that you love me. The plan is still in place. Go do it." Having full confidence in God's love, Peter did it. He became that rock that Jesus promised. At Pentecost, he preached boldly before thousands. About three thousand people were added to the faith that day (see Acts 2:41). From there, he became a leader of the early Church.

Like I said, I do not understand everything about God's omniscience. I know that He does not cause everything to happen. I know that He does not prefer everything that happens. God does not want any of us to suffer. But I also know that He is not surprised by anything that does happen, nor is He let down by any of it. According to Scripture, He directs our steps (see Psalm 37:23). It also promises that He corrects our missteps (see Romans 8:28). The ins and outs of how that works are beyond me. I just know that somehow, despite our failures *and* because of them, He gets each of us right where we are meant to be.

Truth #3: You Cannot Out-Sin God's Love

For me to believe that I am loved without exception, I had to come to terms with the truth of forgiveness. Not so much about past stuff but about present and future stuff. That took some time. A lot of time, really. Mostly because it went against everything I was taught by religion since my "pray Jesus" days. I was raised to believe that forgiveness of each sin happens *after* confession of it. In that tradition, it was confession to a priest. When I left that tradition, it was confession to God. Scripture appeared to leave no room for doubt. The apostle John instructed, "But if we confess our sins to him, he is faithful and just to forgive us our sins and to cleanse us from all wickedness" (1 John 1:9).

To an analytic, linear thinking person like me, the implications of this verse went something like this: *If you do not confess each sin, you are unforgiven of it. And if you are unforgiven, then are you really loved? How can God unconditionally love someone He has something against?* This kind of reasoning is probably why most days I felt like the kid who picks one flower petal for each "He loves me, He loves me not." Whether I would land on loved or unloved was basically a guess. That is how it is when you link God's favor, forgiveness, or love to any kind of performance. Since you cannot do anything perfectly, you are left to wonder or worry where you stand.

As it relates to confession, I could not confess every sin perfectly. You cannot, either. That is not because you and I are rabid sinners. It is because we live as humans in a fallen world. Even if we succeed to sin less and less and less, on this side of eternity, we cannot get down to zero. And we cannot remember everything. I worried what would happen to me, if, God forbid, I died with an unconfessed sin. What if I had a bad thought or forgot to mention something in the hour or two since I prayed last? That might sound neurotic, even morbid, but not all that unreasonable if eternity is on the line. As it turns out, I am not the only neurotic out there. Many people have asked me the same question.

What, then, do we make of John's instruction? He provides a clue in the preceding verse. "If we claim we have no sin, we are only fooling ourselves and not living in the truth" (verse 8). Who claims to be sinless? Not a real Christian. The basis of salvation is our awareness of our need for Jesus because of sin. That has never been up for debate. Though some tried to debate it back then. They were called Gnostics. They professed to believe in Jesus, yet among many of their false teachings, they denied the reality of sin. It is to these people that John gives the instruction of confession. Essentially, he says, "Hey, Gnostics! Rather than denying your sin, why not just admit it and be cleansed of it once and for all?"[3]

Simply put, John's instruction describes salvation, not case-by-case or sin-by-sin forgiveness. Suggesting otherwise puts it at odds with what everyone else said in the New Testament. Remember, John the Baptist boasted that Jesus came to take away the sin of the world (see John 1:29). Paul revealed that because of the cross, God no longer counts people's sins against them (see 2 Corinthians 5:19). The author of Hebrews affirmed that Jesus' sacrifice removed sin once and for all (see Hebrews 9:28).

Thankfully, we do not have to assume that John understood this; we know that he did. He said so just three verses later: "He himself is the sacrifice that atones for our sins—and not only our sins but the sins of all the world" (1 John 2:2). It, of course, is fine, even healthy, to talk to God about your failures. I still do. Just know that when you do, they are already forgiven.

I can hear the critics as I write. "That's hyper grace!" they shout, a few with pitchforks in their hands. Have you heard that phrase before? I hesitate to put it in your mind. But you are bound to come across it if you have not already. "Hyper grace" is the derogatory phrase that some legalists (possibly even some well-meaning people) use to mean the kind of grace that absolves everything—past, present, and future—by faith in Jesus alone, without asking for it or working for it.

Yet, it is ignorant to use this phrase critically because grace is hyper by Scripture's own definition of it. John boasted, "For from [Christ's] fullness we have all received, grace upon grace" (John 1:16 ESV). That sounds hyper to me. Paul affirmed that it is. "As people sinned more and more, God's wonderful grace became more abundant" (Romans 5:20). The Greek word for "more abundant" is *hyperperisseuō*.[4] See the first five letters in that word? They spell "hyper." It means that God's grace is greater. Greater than your feelings. Greater than your fears. Greater than the devil. Greater than sin. Greater than everything. As I said in the last chapter, we better hope that it is. It is our only hope.

I understand that some will misinterpret this as encouragement to sin. People always have. There is nothing new about naysayers, except for their names. Jesus had the Pharisees and the Sadducees; we have *wouldn't-sees* and *couldn't-sees*. The best I can do is echo how Paul responded to similar accusations: "Should we keep on sinning so that God can show us more and more of his wonderful grace? Of course not!" (Romans 6:1–2).

Of course not. Can't get much clearer than that. But when you do—when you inevitably fall short—grace assures that sin does not change God's mind about you. It does not change God's love for you. You cannot out-sin God's unfailing love. I suppose, to some, that is the scandal of it. Like the older brother in the parable of the prodigal son, they see it as unfair that someone could squander the Father's blessings on licentious living, yet still be welcomed home as if none of it ever happened. Welcomed home with a party, no less.

It took me many years to see it, but therein lies the empowerment of love. Rather than the Father lingering on or emphasizing what you do wrong, He celebrates what is right, which is you as His beloved. Maybe that is counter-intuitive to everything human, but isn't that what has worked from the beginning? Isn't that what brought Adam and Eve out of hiding? Isn't that what was at the foundation of David's confidence? Isn't that what emboldened Peter to fulfill his calling?

This brings me to my final encouragement when it comes to accepting God's love. After a failure—when you know that you have blown it, when you have done that thing you hate yet again—as quickly as you can, remember, "God loves me." As weird as it feels, say it aloud, too. And it *will* feel weird. Probably wrong, especially at first. The enemy is sure to make you feel like a thief, as though you are getting something for nothing. I guess you are. But do not wait for enough time to feel like it. Do not wait to do something to try to deserve it. Say it right away; believe it right away. Why not say it now? *God loves me!* A mind and mouth focused on God's love and grace is key to restoration in every area of your life. That is a great topic with which to finish this book. Let's explore it in the final chapter.

QUESTIONS FOR PERSONAL REFLECTION

1. In terms of feeling God's love, where do you fall on the scale between fully feeling it and not feeling it at all? How have your beliefs played a role in that?

2. Describe how the truth of God's omniscience made you feel before reading this book. How has that changed now?

3. What have you believed disappoints God about you or your behavior? Take a moment to imagine Jesus speaking lovingly into those areas.

4. When you think about your future sins being forgiven, do you want to sin more or less? Why or why not?

5. In what ways might contemplating God's unconditional love empower you to strive less, stress less, and sin less?

13

Living from Rest

Let God transform you into a new person by changing the way you think. —Romans 12:2

The pain did not come on strong at first. I had warnings for months, maybe on and off for a year before it got debilitating. But I just chalked up the increasing stiffness and soreness to my morning workouts. In fact, I considered it a sign of progress, even a badge of honor. Since I began working out in my early twenties, I joked with friends that I lived sore. I thought that ignoring and pushing through pain was part of the process.

Silliness. The number of times that I had to hobble up in a hunched position from a dinner table like an old man should not have been ignored. Neither should the feeling of waking up with my lower back half on fire, half being stabbed with knives, also been ignored. Yet it was. I foolishly ignored the symptoms until I could not stand for even ten minutes without agony.

Now, do you suppose that level of stubbornness schedules a doctor's appointment right away? Hardly. That level of stubbornness waits it out, believing it will get better on its own. Some things do, I guess. But this didn't. A month away from the gym made no difference. Two months later, things were worse. By that time, I could not walk or stand for five minutes without wanting to scream or cry. That is when I entered a self-diagnosing phase with the assistance of Dr. YouTube. I tried this exercise and that exercise. This anti-inflammatory medicine and that one. Nothing worked, not in the slightest.

A whole four months in—*four months*—this stubborn me finally surrendered to the aid of a real, live physical therapist. And it was a big, white-flag wave of surrender. I felt completely helpless on my own. The doctor did not even have to see me. Within minutes of a phone call, he knew exactly what to prescribe based only on what I described. My brain needed to be retrained.

In sharing the gist of my situation, please bear in mind that this is only my story, not advice on how to deal with any aches or ailments you may have. As I understand it, due to almost fifteen years of amateur weight training and many more years of sitting behind a computer for eight hours a day, my body had developed some bad habits. Consequently, when I performed basic activities such as standing, bending, or squatting, the wrong muscles fired and eventually over-compensated for others, resulting in the pain and stiffness. In my case, time and self-directed exercises could not ease my symptoms—because the underlying problem was in my brain. It is what was directing my muscles in this wrong manner because that is what it had learned over the years.

That makes enough sense to me, although I was skeptical of the prescription at first. The doctor emailed me a handful of video links with protocols to follow each morning. Most of them asked me to contract a certain muscle for a few seconds before I made a small movement with my leg. Keeping that muscle contracted, I made the movement. Then, after the movement, I was to keep the muscle contracted for a few more seconds. In theory, repeating this numerous times over a period of weeks would reprogram my brain to activate the correct muscles for the basic movements of daily life.

The theory worked. Despite little effort on my part, except for thinking about the muscles and then gently moving each morning, it worked. After a week, I was able to stand without pain. After two weeks, I was back to walking the theme parks (which are no small walks, by the way).

Here is the kicker. It would be wonderful to report that this was a permanent fix. But the pain came back. It came back eight or nine months later after an intense season of writing. Not as badly, but just as frustrating. Environment, gravity, natural tendencies, and long days hunched over a computer took their toll yet again. My muscles slipped back into bad habits, simple as that. Thankfully, the solution was as simple as the last time. A week or two of retraining my brain to fire the right muscles at the right times worked. It never fails to work.

You have learned a lot about me throughout this book. But I have never shared a story only for the fun of it. This one, too, has a point. It reflects the realities of life and God's design for us, both physically and spiritually. This includes the truth of how environment shapes the mind, how the mind influences the body, and the essence of what the apostle

Paul said is the way of restoration: "Let God transform you into a new person by changing the way you think" (Romans 12:2). Most people know this verse as the "renewing of your mind" (NIV). There is value in both expressions. I like the word *renewing* because it gets to the heart of what happens. To renew something means to resume it back to its original, default position after an interruption.[1]

We will get to how that works. But first, it is important to recall your default position.

Your Default Position

You were made for Eden. We all were. Humankind was formed out of the ground of Eden and designed to live there. Like seeds in the right soil with the right sunlight and water, when we are in the place for which we were created, our lives grow and thrive naturally. The actual Garden of Eden, of course, is long gone. Yet it becomes possible for each of us to live there today when you recall that Eden means "God's delight."[2]

Spiritually, Eden is a place of relating to God as pure love and pure grace. It is a place unaffected by sin. It is a place of permanent rest, void of the need to strive. It is the place that Jesus died to restore us to (see Hebrews 4:3).

How? For starters, Jesus came to change your mind about God. Mark recorded that Jesus began His ministry by announcing, "Repent and believe in the gospel" (Mark 1:15 ESV). What does that have to do with changing your mind about God? Everything. I know that *repent* is often described as the means to get God to change His mind about you, usually involving sobbing and sorrow. That is so unfortunate. First, because God's mind never needed to be changed about you.

Nor will it. You were made in His image; He has always had good and loving thoughts toward you. Second, because *repent* does not mean to do something to change God's mind. It is the Greek word for "change your mind."[3]

In the purest sense of the word, Jesus launched His ministry declaring, "I have come to change your mind about God." To what? "Your Father loves you." Everything Jesus did demonstrated that. Everything He taught revealed that. His parables challenged people consistently with that perspective of God. Isn't that the main point of the parable of the prodigal son? Everything that the Holy Spirit does today continues to show it, too. God's love and grace are the heart of the Gospel, the means of entering and maintaining a relationship of intimacy with Him, and the means of any real change.

While God's love will continue to transform you all throughout your life, the ultimate change happened upon your initial acceptance of His love through Jesus. You became a new person (see 2 Corinthians 5:17). While I am in the habit of defining words in this chapter, will you allow me one more? It is a favorite of mine for good reason. *Regeneration* is the theological term for "becoming new."[4] The first six letters of that word spell something that illustrates what happened upon your belief. Do you see *re-gene* in there? This means a complete change in your spiritual DNA, your identity. As your old sinful nature was cut out and crucified with Christ, you were infused with the nature of God so that you are righteous and holy, just as He is (see Romans 6:6; Colossians 2:11; Ephesians 4:24; 1 John 4:17).

Don't miss that: *you are as He is.* This is more than a covering. His identity is not like some spiritual force field that surrounds and protects you as long as you do not accidentally slip out of it. There is no slipping out of Christ. You are in Him and He is in you, united together in a way that cannot be separated. The Bible calls this being "hidden with Christ" (Colossians 3:3). And it is what a *re-geneing* accomplishes. That truth alone should put you at rest. It is why you are not in need of self-improvement or fixing. Not for God's sake, at least. Who you are as you are is as right as you can be, as pleasing to God as you can be, and as complete as you can be.

What is more, since you are in Him, you are also where He is, which Paul revealed is seated in heaven (see Ephesians 2:6). To be seated is the ultimate position of rest. Not only because it sounds relaxing. There is profound historical significance to this idea, which Paul clearly intended to elicit in his original readers. You see, under the old covenant, there was no seat in the temple where the priest offered sacrifices daily for people's sins.

Does that seem strange to you? Considering all the intricate details of the temple, how could it be missing something as basic as a seat? It was not a forgotten detail. The reason the priest could not sit is because the work was never done. The priest had to stand because there was always more sin to atone for, more sacrifices to make (see Hebrews 10:11).

But Jesus finished the work. His announcement from the cross—"It is finished!"—declared the fulfillment of the Law, the end of sin being held against people, and humankind's reconciliation with God. Through Christ, God's plan of restoration is complete. To that end, Jesus offered Himself as the final sacrifice. There is no need for another one. Not from Him; not from you. What kind of sacrifice could have greater impact than that of the Son of God?

It would be stunningly naïve (and bold) to believe that you could offer something more effective. If not even the blood of bulls and goats could do it, then more grief, more giving, more Bible study, more time with God cannot, either. Whatever you can name, nothing is as effective at removing sin, bringing you close to God, and putting you at peace with Him as the sacrifice of our High Priest, Jesus.

So Jesus took a seat. Having finished the work, "He sat down in the place of honor at God's right hand" (verse 12). And as one hidden in Christ, Scripture assures that your real self—your spirit—is already at rest with Him. But what about the part of you that you see, hear, think, and feel with? What about the part of you that interacts with other people? This is the part of you called the flesh. Obviously, this part of you is not in heaven. And that is why it does not enter rest so automatically. It must be taught to rest. That is what the renewing of the mind does. We are getting to the how, but next, you must understand why your flesh gets out of sync with your spirit.

The Interruptions of the Flesh

We live in a fallen world where things routinely slip out of their God-designed function and order. Few things remind me of this more starkly than when that back pain flares up. I know that God did not design me in my late thirties to hobble around like an old man. As I discovered through physical therapy, I know that He designed my mind and muscles to work correctly so that I do not experience pain from something as natural as standing or walking. Yet it happens. Because of various factors, my body forgets to operate as it was designed and it either picks up bad habits or reverts to old habits. Cue the stiffness. Cue the pain.

The stress, frustration, and unrest we intensely feel sometimes happen for the same reason. Not because God is not good. Not because you are not good with God. At the risk of sounding repetitive, as a Christian, you no longer have a sin nature. In other words, you being a sinner is not the problem, because you are not a sinner. Even though you still sin, "sinner" is not your identity. Your default is righteous in Christ. Your real position is at rest—your seat secured with supernatural super glue at the feet of Jesus, who sits at the right hand of God. I will say it again: *you* are not the problem.

So what is the problem? The patterns of the fallen world upon and in your flesh. You cannot escape the influence of them. Not even if you avoid movie theaters, secular music, public schools, and certain news networks. Part of this has to do with science. Your environment began to program your brain before you could ever make a conscious choice. As a child, everything you saw, heard, felt, tasted, and touched shaped your mind almost instantly.

When you experienced something repetitively, your brain created a pathway. This still happens as an adult, but slower. It is how you picked up language and music and math (some of us better than others, clearly). It determines how you see things and how you process information. Scientists have learned that the more experiential something is, the more quickly a pathway is made and the more entrenched it is.[5] That is how you learn to avoid things that hurt you. Like a hot stove top. Or a daddy. Or a church.

That is how I learned to avoid anything that might lead to rejection, including being myself. Due to consistent shunning by peers for my natural interests, strengths, and weaknesses, I built my walls to keep people away. I also discovered that I could perform in ways that kept people focused on other things. But if someone somehow got close enough (or loud enough) with a similar word or action from the past, one of those pathways would regurgitate an old fear or thought. Then, for at least a moment (usually days or weeks), I would forget who I am in Christ, and feel and react as one who is not safe, secure, or loved.

I know that I wrote that in past tense, as if this no longer happens. Do not believe for a second that I am immune from the patterns of the world and all the stinkin' thinkin' it can influence. Trust me, I am not.

I am also not immune from the tricks of the enemy. Let's not forget that he is a very real foe behind some of our unrest. Albeit a defeated foe—we must also remember that. While he undoubtedly exists, too many Christians live fearfully, believing that the devil has unrestricted access to do whatever he wants with them. So much of today's spiritual-warfare teaching is based on this fallacy. It teaches people to do all kinds of spiritual jumping jacks so that the enemy has no right to them.

Talk about exhausting. The truth is, however, as a believer, the enemy already has no right to you. Jesus shut the door to that at the cross (see Colossians 2:15). Besides, the devil cannot even find you. Your real life is hidden in Christ, remember. That is why the enemy shouts. His voice is the only way he can influence you. Through accusations, lies, and slander, he attempts to manipulate your mind so that you forget who you are and what you have in Christ. That is all the power he has.

That, of course, can still be powerful. And as I said, I still hear his lies and slander. They can still trigger thoughts that make me feel and react negatively. The difference between now and years ago is that I have learned the source of these thoughts so that I do not as easily slip into prove, perform, or pretend mode. From wherever they originate, I know that though the thoughts are in me, they are not me. Neither are the reactions they provoke. My flesh and all the attitudes, emotions, and actions it produces are not me. That is why they will not go to heaven with me (see Philippians 3:21).

That is the same for you. The pain you feel, the struggles you face, the mistakes you make—they might come from some place inside of you, but you must know that they are not you. They do not define you. That is why the way to experience peace and rest in a way that you can feel is to remember who you truly are.

How to Put Yourself at Rest

When it comes to my back, no amount of exercise or medicine accomplishes what the occasional retraining of my brain does. Again, this is not medical advice. But as I have explained all throughout this book, our bodies reflect spiritual principles. My story illustrates the transformation that comes from mind renewal, or "changing the way you think" (Romans 12:2).

You might also think of this concept as teaching your thoughts the truth. That is how Paul put it in his second letter to the Corinthians. They had a history of battling the flesh, which comes as no surprise if you know much about the larger Corinthian culture. It was inundated with carnality, somehow even with no smartphones or internet. Apparently, not everyone in the Corinthian church escaped the culture's influence. Paul acknolwedged that though we walk in the flesh physically, we do not deal with it through human methods and willpower. He stressed that we should teach rebellious thoughts the truth of Christ (see 2 Corinthians 10:5).

The way to do that is not with dos and don'ts. That is evident throughout his letter to the Corinthians, but it is also evident as you read his other letters, parts of which we explored in earlier chapters. So what is the way? To the Ephesians, he wrote, "Put on your new nature" (Ephesians 4:24). To the Romans, he said, "Clothe yourself with . . . Christ" (Romans 13:14). To the Colossians, he urged, "Clothe yourselves with love" (Colossians 3:14). To the Philippians, he encouraged, "Fix your thoughts on what is true, and honorable, and right, and pure, and lovely, and admirable" (Philippians 4:8).

These are all various ways to tell us to think about God's love and grace and who we are because of it. In time, this helps us to see according to grace. And hear according to grace. And live according to grace. What does this look like in everyday life? It looks like speaking truth to the symptoms of lies such as fear, insecurity, discouragement, and shame as soon as you recognize them.

Believe it or not, this is something I have had to do while writing every one of my books, including this one. What happens while writing is kind of like what happens when you spray for pests. Many of the ugly critters that you did not know existed come out. Hopefully they come out to die, but they come out, nonetheless. Insecurities often surface that sound like "Who are you to write on this topic?" or "People will reject you if you share that story."

There also comes a point when the pressure of the deadline makes me think that I do not have enough to say, nor enough time to say it. Crippling anxiety can arise from thoughts like these. And you cannot work those away. You must believe them away. In these moments, I remember truths about myself like, "I am clean and complete" or "I am approved and accepted in Christ." I remember truths about God such as, "God is good; He is with me; He is for me." Often, it takes a set or two of repetitions for my mind to snap back to reality and my flesh to follow suit. But it works.

You might find it helpful to search for a Bible verse related to whatever you face. When you find one, read it, then think about it. I like to paraphrase a Bible verse in a way that is personal to me or to my situation. I find that this process helps me identify with or "put on" the truth of it. Just be sure to choose grace-based verses. For all the reasons we covered in this book, don't focus on anything law based.

"God loves me" may be the best place to begin. I am convinced you could go on muttering that under your breath for the rest of your life and handle whatever life throws at you. My friend Susie Larson found that to be true. She shares openly about a history of sexual trauma, Lyme disease, and a neurological disorder. I cannot imagine the mind games those issues provoke. Yet she raised a family, wrote more than twenty books, and continues to host a daily radio show through it all. I had her on my podcast to have her share her secret to prevailing through pain. "Remembering that God loves me," is what she said. She shared that, for a time, she found it helpful to speak, "God loves me" as often as she thought, "God, I love You."[6]

I believe strongly in speaking truth, too. Not that it is required for mind renewal, but it sure is helpful. After all, speaking is a consistent theme in Scripture. Israel's practice of meditation involved speaking. Prayers of blessing were often spoken over people. Jesus taught that speaking to circumstances can change them (see Mark 11:23). And from a scientific perspective, our bodies seem designed to react to the spoken word. Psychologists find that speaking the same idea consistently helps it "stick" far more than rereading it. That comes down to the formation of those pathways I spoke about earlier.[7] I explore that much further in my book *Shut Up, Devil*.

Having said all of this, I must caution you not to make a law out of mind renewal. Whenever this (or any other principle) becomes a *must do*, you have left the sure foundation of God's love and will be prone to all the nasty effects of striving. While there are scientific reasons why changing your thoughts works, the real work takes place in the spirit. As Paul emphasized, it is God who does the transformation (see Romans 12:2; Ephesians 4:23). In His own way and in His own time, He changes you from the inside out by syncing your flesh with the realities of who you are and what you have in Him, truth by truth.

That is my story. And it is an ongoing story. It will be for you, too. God will continue to bring you to fresh insights about His goodness and love that will heal, deliver, and change you in all kinds of ways. But as you wait for Him to do what only He can do, rest in His grace. Because of Jesus, you have nothing to prove, you have nothing to earn, and you have nothing to fix. What matters most is that God is good and that you are good with God, just as you are.

On that point, I will leave you with one of the truths I have received that gave me the most rest. It came in a movie theater, of all places. I was there to see yet another portrayal of Jesus' crucifixion. As you would expect from a story about the cross, the movie had plenty of good lines. But what put me at ease did not come from the movie. It came out of a frustration.

The problem was the speakers. From the beginning, there was an awful crackle sound from them, like someone was wadding up paper slowly. The noise made it difficult to concentrate. I had hoped it would work itself out within a few minutes. It didn't. Fifteen minutes in, I decided that somebody ought to tell a manager. And that somebody would be me. I also decided that I would tell them to give me a refund or a voucher for the trouble.

I never got that far. In fact, I only got as far as a few seats down when, in my mind, I heard, *My story is always told through imperfect speakers.* No refund needed. Nothing more to say. I sat right back down. And I have been seated ever since.

QUESTIONS FOR PERSONAL REFLECTION

1. Which of the realities about your "default position" in Christ is most liberating to you, and why?

2. What are some of the most common thoughts that attempt to interrupt your "default position" in Christ?

3. Using everything you now know, what truths can you personalize to counter those negative thoughts?

4. Looking back on your life, what truths has God led you to that have changed you the most so far? How did He lead you to them?

5. Reflecting upon everything you have discovered in this book, what is your greatest takeaway? How will it influence your life?

Acknowledgments

Sir Winston Churchill is credited as having once said, "Writing a book is an adventure. To begin with it is a toy and an amusement. Then it becomes a mistress, then it becomes a master, then it becomes a tyrant. The last phase is that just as you are about to be reconciled to your servitude, you kill the monster and fling him to the public."

This book is the product of such an adventure. It is also the product of those who stood with me (some in person, others in spirit) through every step of the adventure, from the tinkering of ideas to the throes of writing to "flinging to the public."

There is the team at Chosen Books, especially Kim Bangs and David Sluka. You recognized the magnitude of this message from the start. Thank you for your advocacy and for helping me hone it, polish it, and spread it.

Speaking of polishing, there is Lori Janke, my editor. You did it once again! You have made the message better—and me, too. Thank you!

There are the partners of Kyle Winkler Ministries. Your generosity and prayers helped to produce yet another tool of hope and healing. You share in the reward of those impacted by this book. Thank you!

There are my Orlando friends who joined me for breakfasts, lunches, dinners, ice cream outings, and days at Disney. You each know who you are. You demonstrate the way of grace so well. You brought laughter, sanity, encouragement, and hope at all the right moments and milestones of this adventure. Thank you!

Few know more about what this book means to me than my family. Few also know my imperfections more. Thank you for loving me just as I am. Thank you for supporting who God has made me to be.

Notes

Chapter 1 The Divine Design

1. Alex Krumer, "Why Do Top Athletes Choke Under Pressure?" Psychology Today, February 11, 2022, https://www.psychologytoday.com/us/blog/sports-and-psychology/202202/why-do-top-athletes-choke-under-pressure.

2. Alyson Meister and Maude Lavanchy, "The Science of Choking Under Pressure," *Harvard Business Review*, April 7, 2022, https://hbr.org/2022/04/the-science-of-choking-under-pressure.

3. "What the Bible Says About Garden of Eden," BibleTools.org, 2023, https://www.bibletools.org/index.cfm/fuseaction/topical.show/RTD/cgg/ID/3513/Garden-of-Eden.htm.

Chapter 2 Why Diets Don't Work

1. Allison Lau, "The Rise of Fad Diets," CNBC Make It, January 11, 2021, https://www.cnbc.com/video/2021/01/11/how-dieting-became-a-71-billion-industry-from-atkins-and-paleo-to-noom.html.

2. Meg Selig, "Why Diets Don't Work . . . and What Does," Psychology Today, October 21, 2010, https://www.psychologytoday.com/us/blog/changepower/201010/why-diets-dont-work-and-what-does.

3. Alissa Rumsey, "The Science Behind Why Diets Don't Work," Alissa Rumsey.com, December 3, 2021, https://alissarumsey.com/why-not-to-go-on-a-diet/.

4. Amy Nordrum, "The New D.A.R.E. Program—This One Works," *Scientific American*, September 10, 2014, https://www.scientificamerican.com/article/the-new-d-a-r-e-program-this-one-works/.

5. Shaunacy Ferro, "The Science of PSAs: Do Anti-Drug Ads Keep Kids Off Drugs?," Popular Science, April 15, 2013, https://www.popsci.com/science/article/2013-03/science-psas-do-anti-drug-ads-keep-kids-drugs/.

6. Nordrum, "New D.A.R.E. Program."

7. Rumsey, "Why Diets Don't Work."

8. Edward Sullivan, "Focus on the Snow, Not on the Trees," Medium, October 27, 2016, https://medium.com/@edwardsullivan/focus-on-the-snow-not-on-the-trees-f95515fb51bb.

Chapter 3 Get a New God

1. Liana Finck, "In This Time of War, I Propose We Give Up on God," *New York Times*, April 15, 2022, https://www.nytimes.com/2022/04/15/opinion/passover-giving-up-god.html.

2. Richard Dawkins, *The God Delusion* (Boston: Mariner, 2006), 31.

3. Dawkins, 15.

4. A.W. Tozer, *The Knowledge of the Holy* (San Francisco: HarperOne, 2009), 1.

5. Kyle Winkler, *Shut Up, Devil* (Minneapolis: Chosen, 2022), 16.

6. Dawkins, 31.

7. Shawna Dolansky, "How the Serpent in the Garden Became Satan," Bible History Daily, January 31, 2023, https://www.biblicalarchaeology.org/daily/biblical-topics/bible-interpretation/how-the-serpent-in-the-garden-became-satan/.

8. "Spiritual Meaning of the Name John (Revealed)," Let's Learn Slang, accessed September 9, 2023, https://letslearnslang.com/spiritual-meaning-of-the-name-john/.

Chapter 4 What Did Jesus Do?

1. Doug Hershey, "Hebrew Meaning of Holy – Set Apart for a Purpose," Fellowship of Israel Related Ministries, February 7, 2016, https://firmisrael.org/learn/hebrew-meaning-holy-set-apart-for-purpose/.

2. Dr. Alan L. Gillen, "Biblical Leprosy: Shedding Light on the Disease that Shuns," Answers In Genesis, June 10, 2007, https://answersingenesis.org/biology/disease/biblical-leprosy-shedding-light-on-the-disease-that-shuns/.

3. Andrew Robert M.A., D.D., "Definition for Face," Bible History Online, 2023, https://bible-history.com/faussets/f/face.

4. "Love," *Merriam-Webster*, 2023, www.merriam-webster.com/dictionary/love.

5. For a step-by-step commentary on Jesus' interaction with the woman at the well, see chapter 7 of my book *Shut Up, Devil: Silencing the 10 Lies behind Every Battle You Face.*

Chapter 5 The God Who Is on Your Side

1. "Paraclete," Bible Study Tools, 2023, https://www.biblestudytools.com/dictionary/paraclete/.

2. R. C. Sproul, "The Paraclete," *Ligonier*, January 17, 2022, https://www.ligonier.org/podcasts/ultimately-with-rc-sproul/the-paraclete.

3. Preston Sprinkle, "Love Your . . . Enemies?" Theology in the Raw, August 31, 2016, https://theologyintheraw.com/love-your-enemies/.

4. Robert Louis Wilken, *The First Thousand Years: A Global History of Christianity* (New Haven/London: Yale University Press, 2012), 65–66.

5. "Paideuō," BlueLetterBible.org, 2023, https://www.blueletterbible.org/lexicon/g3811/kjv/tr/0-1/.

Chapter 6 The Key to Intimacy

1. "Charisma-G5486," Blue Letter Bible, 2023, https://www.blueletterbible.org/lexicon/g5486/kjv/tr/0-1/.

2. Chad Brand, Charles Draper, Archie England, *Holman Illustrated Bible Dictionary* (Nashville: Holman Publishing, 2003), *Scribd.com*, 2213.

Chapter 7 What God Wants Most

1. J. Jeremias, *The Prayers of Jesus* (Naperville: Allenson, 1967).

2. David Neff, "Biblical Adoption Is Not What You Think It Is," *Christianity Today*, November 22, 2013, https://www.christianitytoday.com/ct/2013/december/heirs-biblicaliblical-take-on-adoption.html.

3. Caroline Bologna, "What People Call Their Moms and Dads in Other Countries," HuffPost, June 7, 2018, https://www.huffpost.com/entry/what-people-call-their-moms-and-dads-in-other-countries_n_5b1167d2e4b02143b7ccobaa.

4. Paul Y. Hoskisson, "Why Is Abba in the New Testament?," *Religious Educator* 6, *no.* 1 (2005): 43–49.

Chapter 8 Enough Is Enough

1. Fresh Air, "Tom Hanks Says Self-Doubt Is 'A High-Wire Act That We All Walk,'" NPR, April 26, 2016, https://www.npr.org/2016/04/26/475573489/tom-hanks-says-self-doubt-is-a-high-wire-act-that-we-all-walk.

2. I tell this story in my book *Silence Satan: Shutting Down the Enemy's Attacks, Threats, Lies, and Accusations* (Lake Mary, FL: Charisma House, 2014).

3. Kyle Winkler, *Shut Up, Devil* (Minneapolis: Chosen Books, 2022), 80.

4. Got Questions Ministries, "Summary of the Book of Colossians," Got Questions Ministries, 2023, https://www.gotquestions.org/Book-of -Colossians.html.

5. Tiffany Ayuda, "How the Japanese art of Kintsugi Can Help You Deal With Stressful Situations," NBC News Digital, April 28, 2018, https://www .nbcnews.com/better/health/how-japanese-art-technique-kintsugi-can -help-you-be-more-ncna866471.

Chapter 9 Designed to Be Different

1. Chris Drew, "22 Aspects of Identity," The Helpful Professor, June 8, 2023, https://helpfulprofessor.com/aspects-of-identity/.

2. Discovery Eye Foundation, "The Optic Nerve and Its Visual Link to the Brain," Discovery Eye Foundation, March 12, 2015, https://discovery eye.org/optic-nerve-visual-link-brain/.

Chapter 10 Ending Your Battle with Sin

1. Ferdinand Pauwels, "Martin Luther's Spiritual Practice Was Key to the Success of the Reformation," The Conversation, October 24, 2017, https://theconversation.com/martin-luthers-spiritual-practice-was-key -to-the-success-of-the-reformation-83340.

2. Catholic Encyclopedia, "Stylites (Pillar Saints)," New Advent, 2021, https://www.newadvent.org/cathen/14317b.htm.

3. Strong's Concordance, "2398. Chata," Bible Hub, 2023, https://bible hub.com/hebrew/2398.htm.

4. Ted Shimer, "How Porn is Rewiring the Brains of a Generation," RELEVANT, November 2, 2022, https://relevantmagazine.com/life5/porn -is-rewiring-a-whole-generation-christians-included/.

5. Luke Gilkerson, "The Apostle Paul: 5 Secrets to Fighting Sexual Sin," Covenant Eyes, March 1, 2023, https://www.covenanteyes.com/2014/10 /31/apostle-pauls-secret-fighting-sexual-sin/.

6. Andrew Farley, "The Power of Grace to Overcome Sin," *The Shut Up, Devil Show* video, 13:02, February 21, 2023, https://www.kylewinkler.org /videos/conversations/power-of-grace-to-overcome-sin-andrew-farley/.

7. Mike Szczensny, "Spread the Love," *Resounding the Faith*, 2023, https://resoundingthefaith.com/2018/03/17/%E2%80%8Egreek-ἐνδύω -enduo/.

Chapter 11 The Ground of Growth

1. Penn Medicine, "Can You Kiss and Hug Your Way to Better Health? Research Says Yes," Penn Medicine, January 8, 2018, https://www.penn

medicine.org/updates/blogs/health-and-wellness/2018/february/affec tion.

Chapter 12 How to Accept God's Love

1. "Disappointed," *New Oxford American Dictionary* (New York: Oxford University Press, 2019).

2. Jack Wellman, "Apostle Peter Biography: Timeline, Life, and Death," What Christians Want to Know, 2023, https://www.whatchristianswant toknow.com/apostle-peter-biography-timeline-life-and-death/.

3. Andrew Farley, *The Naked Gospel* (Grand Rapids: Zondervan, 2009), 151–153.

4. "Hyperperisseuō," Blue Letter Bible, 2023, https://www.blueletter bible.org/lexicon/g5248/niv/mgnt/0-1/.

Chapter 13 Living from Rest

1. "Renew," Dictionary.com, 2023, https://www.dictionary.com/browse /renew.

2. "What the Bible Says About Garden of Eden," BibleTools.org, 2023, https://www.bibletools.org/index.cfm/fuseaction/topical.show/RTD/cgg /ID/3513/Garden-of-Eden.htm.

3. "Metanoia, G3341," Blue Letter Bible, 2023, https://www.blueletter bible.org/lexicon/g3341/kjv/tr/0-1/metanoia.

4. "3824, Paliggenesia," Bible Hub, 2023, https://biblehub.com/greek /3824.htm.

5. Debbie Hampton, "The 10 Fundamentals of Rewiring Your Brain," HuffPost, June 17, 2016, https://www.huffpost.com/entry/the-10-funda mentals-of-re_b_9625926.

6. Susie Larson, "Prevailing Through Pain (The Susie Larson Story)," *The Shut Up, Devil Show* video, 27:01, February 11, 2021, https://www.kyle winkler.org/videos/conversations/prevailing-through-pain-susie-larson -story/.

7. Fit4D, "The Neuroscience of Behavior Change," StartUp Health, August 8, 2017, https://healthtransformer.co/the-neuroscience-of-behavior -change-bcb567fa83c1.

Kyle Winkler is a practical Bible teacher and creator of the popular *Shut Up, Devil!* mobile app. He is known for his vulnerable but bold messages that have been shared on platforms and media throughout the world, including TBN's *Praise the Lord*, *Life Today*, *700 Club Interactive*, Sid Roth's *It's Supernatural!*, *The Blaze*, and many more. To get there, however, he first had to overcome deep wounds of rejection, shame, and insecurity. With God's grace, he did. That is why he is so passionate about helping others experience grace in their own lives.

Kyle holds a Master of Divinity in Biblical Studies from Regent University. He resides in Central Florida. To schedule Kyle to speak at your church or event, please email scheduling@kylewinkler.org.

Connect with Kyle:

kylewinkler.org

- @KyleWinklerMinistries
- @KyleWinklerMinistries
- @KyleJWinkler
- @KyleWinkler